Fashionable
Nihilism

A Critique of
Analytic Philosophy

Bruce Wilshire

State University of New York Press

Published by
State University of New York Press, Albany

© 2002 State University of New York

For information, address State University of New York Press,
90 State Street, Suite 700, Albany, NY 12207

Production by Dana Foote
Marketing by Patrick Durocher

Library of Congress Cataloging-in-Publication Data

Wilshire, Bruce W.
  Fashionable nihilism : a critique of analytic philosophy / Bruce Wilshire.
    p. cm.
  Includes bibliographical references and index.
  ISBN 0-7914-5429-0 (alk. paper) — ISBN 0-7914-5430-4 (pbk. : alk. paper)
  1. Philosophy. 2. Analysis (Philosophy). I. Title.

B29.W496 2002
146'.4—dc21
                                                    2002020822

10 9 8 7 6 5 4 3 2 1

Fashionable
Nihilism

For my Pluralist colleagues, here and there, young and old, and to the memory of my grand teachers at New York University.

There are many things to know in this world, but how to live is the only thing that really matters.

—Leo Tolstoy

Philosophy lives in words, but truth and fact well up in our lives in ways that exceed verbal formulation. There is in the living act of perception always something that glimmers and twinkles and will not be caught, and for which reflection comes too late. No one knows this as well as the philosopher. He must fire his volley of new vocables out of his conceptual shotgun, for his profession condemns him to this industry, but he secretly knows the hollowness and irrelevancy.

—William James

I may know something but insulate the knowledge, as it were . . . live as if it were not there. If knowledge is to bear fruit in us, we must think of it daily . . . [it must] affect me bodily here and now. I know of it, to be sure, when I am asked; but I think there is time. No, there is not much time.

—Karl Jaspers

In those days I was convinced that I sincerely and totally affirmed certain propositions, such as, "The sun is shining." I would have said that my belief in the reality of the sun's shining was complete and unreserved. But the sunlight didn't reach me, didn't suffuse me through and through.

—Anonymous

CONTENTS

PREFACE

What I relate is the history of the next two centuries. I describe
what is coming, what can no longer come differently: *the advent of
nihilism*. . . . Our whole European culture is moving for some
time now, with a tortured tension that is growing from decade to
decade, as toward catastrophe: restlessly, violently, headlong, like a
river that wants to reach the end, that no longer reflects, that is
afraid to reflect.

—Friedrich Nietzsche

Forgetting can move so gradually and by increments so small that we
forget that we have forgotten anything, let alone, of course, what it is
we've forgotten. This has happened, I believe, in many of "the
better" university departments of philosophy. I have assembled this book
in an effort to reflect, to recall myself to remembering. Maybe it will help
others also.

Once, Socrates was a sort of patron saint of philosophers. It was
understood that philosophy was a way of questioning, musing, ruminat-
ing, living—a way of being a person. None of this need ever have taken
written form, assuming that the person even *could* read and write at the
time. Language was spoken, and what was communicated was the presence
of the speaker in the words spoken.

When the immemorial oral tradition tended to be forgotten, philosophy was thought to take any number of written forms: meditation,
dialogue, confession, personal essay, and so on. Now those forms have
pretty well been forgotten, at least in "the better circles." And the forgetting is being forgotten.

We move ever more and more in a kind of self-contented limbo, I
think: a kind of dream of wakefulness and presence. Imagine being
brought up in a room completely lined with mirrors. Imagine also that

one's mobility is so limited that the mirrors cannot be touched. How could one imagine the possibility that one's room is but a small sector of the world?

The metaphor is fantastic, but it may help to crack open the shell of habitual experience and let us see how greatly limited we may be in actual life. In fact, for many professionalized philosophers perennial possibilities for exploration are concealed, and the concealment is concealed. They automatically assume that philosophy must be written in prose—or at least be writable in that form—and that it must be done so in the most impersonal possible way. Philosophy is not exactly science, they think, but it must resemble science in its style and mood of detachment: its appearance of being without any particular person's or any particular group's biases. Even an analytic paper in metaphysics must cast a spell of cool reserve, as if, well, "that's what the concepts dictate, like it or not." Anyone, then, who writes in a personal manner obviously lacks rigor and discipline. Probably an added judgment is made: that person is narcissistic and self-indulgent.

This calls for reflection. The many astounding discoveries of modern science tend to spawn uncritical belief in progress across the whole field of human endeavor. Philosophers, it is thought, were once expected to oversee the development of all knowledge. But now we know, or think we know, that once we formulate issues and methods precisely enough, special fields of investigation drop off from the body of philosophy. The discipline is now so thin that it can barely stand by itself.

It used to be philosophy's province to investigate the soul—but no longer, it is thought. Now we have the sciences of psychology, psychotherapy, sociology, personnel management—and various "rational dispositions of human resources." Philosophers need no longer write the personal essay, say, or the confession; they can cooperate with the progress of science and write their quasi-scientific, personally detached, conceptual analyses of what's left over after other modes of inquiry have taken their bites.

No doubt, particular sciences sometimes contribute mightily to alleviating certain forms of psychopathology, and to rectifying human derangements properly termed clinical. But what happens when philosophers conclude that they need no longer participate personally in what Socrates called "the tendance of the soul"? What happens to our morale, the sustaining sense of our dignity and powers, our worth, our meaning and being as responsible individuals?

I think this uncritical belief in progress promotes a miasmic and pervasive pathology, a pathology so constant and contrastless—so "normal"—that we cannot possibly pigeonhole it in any one or two of the received categories of the sciences. It is what Primo Levi and others discovered in Auschwitz and other places bent on the systematic degradation and destruction of human beings. Levi objected to Bruno Bettelheim's classification of the Nazis' behavior in psychiatric terms—neurotic, psychotic, and so forth. These terms were all artifacts of "the clinical western university." They aided in evading a hard look at the reality of what was happening.

Could this reaction against the personal by philosophers I and others call analytic be, at bottom, one of fear (to recall Nietzsche's word)? Defensiveness? A fear of casting reflection on their own persons? Are many very bright people in philosophy (bright as judged by criteria common in "the better circles" today) blindly afraid of their own precarious identity and unspeakable vulnerability as particular bodily beings caught up in floods of events? Might this be the deepest reason for the now habitual, completely taken for granted, expectation that philosophical reflection always stays at a distance, is always detached, is always converted into a quasi-scientific, analytical paper? Is what Arthur Schopenhauer and, in our day, Gabriel Marcel have described as the inestimable suffering of human life the reason for the endemic shielding, the habitual, constant, and contrastless heavy mist that distances and lulls?

In this distancing, are aspects of our own reality as persons deeply concealed, and the concealment concealed? Are many professors of philosophy today afraid to reflect? I think so.

To many this will seem outrageously counterintuitive. "Philosophers not reflective? Philosophers spend their lives reflecting, and many of them spend their lives reflecting on the self!"

But what if it could be shown that philosophers who function within analytic traditions tend to reflect on self in a way that unwittingly impoverishes and objectifies self in one way or another? With the consequence that we organisms' immediate valuations and emotional involvements in the world, and angles on and in it, are obscured? That is, that the flood of our own actual, personal, lived subjectivity is dimmed down and obscured, self is obscured? I mean the piercing actuality of *one's own self* is obscured; hence, very probably, certain features of any self are lost.

This is what Nietzsche believes. And if his words at the head of this Preface are discounted because they come from his last, questionable work,

Will to Power, words of equivalent force can be cited from his earlier *Untimely Meditations*:

> The proficiency of our finest scholars, their heedless industry, their heads smoking day and night, their very craftsmanship: how often the real meaning of all this lies in the desire to keep something hidden from oneself!

And what if in good conscience we can't pass all this off onto psychiatrists and psychotherapists, specialists presumably in detecting self-deception? Because we strongly suspect that when philosophers believe that the detached, quasi-scientific paper is the only right way to pursue philosophy, they take refuge in a covert religion and ideology.

This suspicion prompts the greatest philosophical issues to burst out. Why have all human cultures, up until some apparent exceptions in the twentieth century, generated and sustained religions? Why is human suffering inestimably great, as Schopenhauer and Marcel put it? Why is self-knowledge so terribly difficult to achieve and to retain? We can still be hounded and hunted by that which hounded and hunted Socrates: the commandment of Apollo—Know thyself!

Kierkegaard, William James, Thoreau, and others I admire are very close to Nietzsche in his condemnation of philosophers who will not or cannot reflect on their own persons: that is, wholly professionalized philosophers. I display grounds for their condemnation in many analytic philosophers' behaviors today. I think that in gradually losing the power of fitting, apt, and determined reflection on one's own self, they lose not just an old-fashioned homey demeanor and atmosphere. They lose an essential condition for self-knowledge. They slide blithely into nihilism.

To recall myself to remembering, and to goad myself to reflection, I have written the essays that follow. Though all but one were written within the last two years, they were not written to compose a book. They just fell into place as a book. A common concern grouped them. The concern is to remember and to hang onto oh-so-close elusive reality. The concern is to avoid the insulated box of impersonal abstractions if I possibly can. Only with the first, most recent essay was I able to say that a book had been forming itself.

The next three essays are historical in one manner or other. One is the recalling—first through William James—of the existential and phenomenological thought indigenous to our own Euro-American thinkers.

This way of thought has been completely occluded by analytic philosophers, those who can practically be defined as being ignorant of their own history, and indeed of most nineteenth and twentieth century philosophy as well. (The exceptions are the figures who can be fitted into analytic philosophy's ossified framework, particularly various logicians or logician-philosophers, for example, Gottlob Frege.)

Aided again by James's thought, I assess the bainful consequences for philosophy and life of depersonalizing and professionalizing philosophy, particularly through the massive grip of the American Philosophical Association. Embedded in our professionalized and commercialized culture, the APA promotes almost inevitably the marketing of persons and ideas. This instead of encouraging and supporting the whole self, the soul, to open up to be cultivated by ideas—perhaps harrowed by them. Rounding out this first section of the book, I include a detailed account of our Pluralist rebellion in the APA, which first erupted in 1978 and holds its course today.

The four essays that follow are more "substantive" than are the "merely historical" ones. (These are scare quotes. I think the distinction drawn between "doing philosophy" and "doing the history of philosophy" is an artifact of analytic philosophers' presumption to transcend history, to speak from a god's eye point of view on "the conceptual realities.") These subsequent essays are my attempts to grasp certain very strange and vexing aspects of human reality: genocidal terrors, manias, and mass movements, as a prime example; or the seemingly bewildering effect of our total cultural environment on the workings of the genes themselves—and the relevance of indigenous thought world-wide to figuring this out; then, reflections on Henry Bugbee's meditations on the sacred significance for our lives of what we don't know we don't know, and his attempt to find himself at home in the unknown.

The ninth and last essay is a personal reflection on the death of my daughter. If thinking philosophically is of no use in enduring the shocks of life, it has lost much of its reason for being, as people have prized it through the ages. I don't expect psychiatrists to solve this "problem" for me.

I

Nihilistic Consequences of
Analytic Philosophy

Only a few days had elapsed since the annual meeting of the American Philosophical Association immediately following Christmas. It was the 2000 meeting, only a year short of the centenary of the Association. The APA is the official professional society for academic philosophers in the United States. It is the official society because, among other things, it is the employment agency for the profession. A colleague in another university sent me this e-mail message:

> I thought you might enjoy this snippet of talk that I overheard in an elevator at the APA. It was a conversation between two young men who are at Princeton (according to nametags) and finishing the graduate program/ going on the job market (according to context): [I came in a couple floors into the conversation]
>
> #*1:* . . . So did the last interview go just as well?
> #*2:* No. It really didn't go well at all. It was very odd. [*puzzled look*]
> #*1:* How so?
> #*2:* Well, for example, they asked me what I would like to teach and I talked about my philosophy of mind course, you know, and one of them cut in and asked me if I would have the students read William James and . . .
> #*1:* William James? The Pragmatist? [*said in disbelief*]
> #*2:* Yes, yes, and so I told them of course not. Can you imagine?
> #*1:* Good. What did they say?
> #*2:* They said, "Why not?"
> #*1:* What did you say?
> #*2:* I said I never read anyone who takes philosophy personally [*look of great distaste*] or confuses philosophy with things that matter in their little lives.

#*1*:   Right. If they want to talk about philosophy as if it matters personally,
          they need to get out of the profession or at least go back to school.
          Yeah—maybe we [Princeton] could get together with Pittsburgh and
          Rutgers and offer some regional postdoctoral remedial programs for
          those kinds of people. [*great snickering and laughter*]

And what is analytic philosophy? Rather than the old standby of
attempting to define by adducing necessary and sufficient conditions for
applying terms, I will try a kind of ostensive procedure. I will point, and
say, "There, that's what I mean." Actual instances of the "analytic" habit of
mind will appear in concrete situations.

Modest contextual or *in situ* clarifications will be gained. We will see
central or paradigmatic instances, but see also where cases might appear on
the margins. In fact, an indefinite number of borderline cases might appear; and with this the complexity, variety, and frequent fuzziness of actual
life-situations is acknowledged.

I point first to the elevator conversation. The second example is the
Leiter Report, or the Gourmet Guide to Analytic Philosophy Departments
in the United States. It has been disseminated for about ten years to
university administrators and philosophy departments, the ones that
count, across the nation. It ranks, it says, analytic departments of philosophy nationwide. It chronicles year by year the horse race for the top spot.
Princeton, Rutgers (my school), Pittsburgh, and at times Harvard and
others, have jockeyed for the lead. Very recently, NYU's newly reminted
doctoral program—reminted with a vengeance—has flashed to the front,
a stunning dark horse.

The criteria for ranking? Its reputation among those who know.
Those in the know simply know, and Brian Leiter knows who these people
are. About one hundred philosophers are asked to rank departments nationwide. Reports circulate of contending departments offering Leiter the
latest news of faculty appointments. Stars being lured; or stars threatening
to leave their old departments because of undisclosed offers; or with
spouses discontented so the two might be movable as a pair; or a star
negotiating for a professorship if he or she is guaranteed a one-course-
a-year teaching load on the graduate level only.

Until very recently, midway through the report Leiter threw in a
completely unfounded claim: The best teaching in Continental philosophy is found in analytic departments. He simply knows. Last year Leiter

really did limit his ranking only to analytic departments.[1] In the semblance of an attempt to supply criteria for his judgments, he distinguishes between departments that offer an historic emphasis, among other emphases, and those that are "problem solving."

A telltale point: Only in the last year have well-known Anglo-American philosophers begun to criticize The Report (coincidentally with a coldly furious letter to the APA Board from the 2000-strong Continental Group, The Society for Phenomenology and Existential Philosophy). Thus Bernard Williams, guest speaking at NYU, scoffed gently at the distinction Leiter draws between studying history of philosophy and "problem solving." For the very idea of what problems are, or what problems there are, stems typically from historical studies, or neglect of same. But the main point is, for about a decade The Report went unchallenged by analytic philosophers, and indeed was relished by quite a few. And not unchallenged harmlessly, for deans have been known to allocate funds and faculty positions on the "objective basis" of The Report. Leiter informs us that the website for the *Philosophical Gourmet Report, 2000–2001,* has received 130,356 "visits" since November 1998.

Now for the third and last exhibit of analytic philosophy to which I point ("I mean *that*"): the new NYU graduate program, which exhibits perhaps the final analysis of analysis. This is a great boon. Seeing where this habit of thought has finally gotten, we can see clearly where it has always tended. In the new program, no dissertation is required for the doctorate, no comprehensive exams (so of course no history of philosophy exam), no foreign languages.[2] Just a few analytic gems, polished, tight exhibits of analytic skill in argumentation, papers publishable in the best journals. And what are they? The ones who publish the best philosophers. An airtight argument, one must admit.

We have all we need to sketch initially the meaning of "analytic philosophy." The consequences for our lives of this habit of thought are intimated.

Return, please, to the Princetonians in the elevator. How explain the hauteur of these young men? The answer to this will supply much of what we need to know about nihilism, and how analytic philosophy encourages it. What enables apparently intelligent and successful graduate students in philosophy (intelligent and successful judged by the standards of a highly commercialized, technologized, and analytic society), what enables them to claim that older philosophers such as myself and my colleagues should be sent back to school at Pittsburgh, Princeton, Rutgers (!), and, I suppose, NYU to be reeducated?

It must be that they observe from a radically ahistorical and modern-progressivist point of view, and that they take it completely for granted. It must be that the tide set in motion by the scientist-philosophers of the seventeenth century—Descartes is the best example—has come full term. But let the subsequent physician-philosopher John Locke epitomize the tide, in fact the tidal wave. The enlightened philosopher is to accept a subordinate position: He must be, says Locke, an "underlaborer" to the empirical scientist.

Undeterred by the Romantic rebellion of the early nineteenth century—and later idealists, pragmatists, and phenomenologists—this tidal wave crashes through the twentieth and twenty-first centuries. Augmented by scientific and technological marvels of these centuries, the wave carries all before it, the whole culture and now much of the world besides.

We best call this tidal wave *scientism*. This is the view that *only* science can know. Scientism cannot be supported by science itself. For to substantiate the claim that other ways of knowing are fraudulent, or at least unreliable, would require that science pursue these putative ways of knowing and determine that they get us nowhere. But to pursue these other ways reliably would require science to abandon its own proven methods and scope of validity. Or, science would be required to rule a priori and arbitrarily that the other ways couldn't possibly be effective in their subject matter areas. Either way, science oversteps itself. Scientism is ideology, not science. The simple fact is, not all questions or issues can be resolved by any single method, scientific or otherwise.

The young men's hauteur is an instance of scientism. Their reasoning (insofar as that term applies at all) must go something like this: Since science progresses, and philosophy is supposed to attach itself somehow to science, philosophy must also progress. Hence, knowledge of the history of philosophy is inessential: where we start from now funds and holds within itself all previous progress. At most, studying the history of philosophy satisfies an antiquarian's curiosity. Hence, as well, an analytic philosopher's knowledge of the history of analytic philosophy itself is inessential.

Hegel put it succinctly: *Wesen ist was ist gewesen.* Being is what has become. Not to know how one has become what one is, means one has a grossly inadequate idea of what one is. The Princeton graduate students pride themselves in never reading "anyone who takes philosophy personally or confuses philosophy with things that matter in their little lives." But being ignorant, apparently, of how they (and their professors, presumably) have come to hold such a view, they have no idea of how it might be criticized, or who they are who hold it. What would Socrates, Kant, Hegel, or James have said about it? Socrates believed that philosophy is tendance of the soul. (Can you imagine him countenancing a "gourmet report"?) Kant knew that one of the essential philosophical questions is, What may I hope? Hegel saw that nothing—but nothing—happens of note in the world without passion. James observed that if one who desires self-knowledge takes exclusively a [supposedly] detached and dispassionate view of oneself, one has already prejudiced what one can be, and, of course, what one can know of oneself.

In fact, one is always personally involved some way in every investigation one undertakes. One is particularly entangled in one's person when denying that one is personally involved. To presume to transcend personal involvement through a quasi-scientific "philosophy of mind" is to be massively self-deceived. Presuming to transcend personal self, these selves group themselves and assert themselves blindly. The damage spreads through everything they touch. In the Maoist manner, those still stuck in the old ways are to be purged or "reeducated."

Who will teach the undergraduates who still take philosophy courses (an ever shrinking number)? In great part it will be these newly minted, or about to be minted, young Ph.D.'s. Those who have no idea of the travail through which humankind has passed, over many, many millennia, in order to become semihumane and semicivilized—at least some of the time. Those graduate students who may say, for example, to their still younger undergraduate charges that existentialism was a mere fad, or a product of the extreme anxiety of the World War II years, or the work of those who never outgrew adolescent identity crises. As if Sartre or Heidegger or William James invented the ideas of death or of identity crisis. As if the main labor of philosophy had not always been to guide us into the fullest possible self-development and self-knowledge, despite anxiety and death—or because of them!

Recall how Socrates in *Phaedo* concludes his arguments for the immortality of the soul. He and his friends conclude that they had at least done their best in engaging a greatly difficult question. But the dialogue doesn't end there. Socrates launches into an extended recounting of ancient myths of the journey of the soul after death, its passage through underground rivers, and so on. Try this yourself with the typical graduate student analytically trained: Ask him or her why Socrates (and Plato) end the dialogue this way. See if you get any intelligent discourse on the immemorial role of myth in the development and constitution of human beings. Typically you will get, at best, a logician's response to the validity of Socrates' earlier arguments, and that's about all. In hearing nothing but the latest in "scientific" philosophy, they have been cheated by their professors.

Nihilism means: to mangle the roots of our thinking-feeling-evaluating selves, to lose the full potential of our immediate ecstatic involvement in the world around us. It means to lose full contact with our willing-feeling-valuing life-projects: to have a shallow sense of what is valuable in human life. It means to be arch, smug, dried out—to be a talking head among other such heads. Speak and reason as we will, we are no longer moved in our depths.

Nietzsche believed we moderns were losing our depth. When we speak, depth is a matter of being present as a person in what we say; it is not just a matter of asserting informational or logical "content." Or, as the apt phrase has it, depth means standing behind what we say. At decisive junctures of life, the authentic person's each word and act is an implicit vow: "I bet my life on this." The nihilist says, in effect, there is nothing worth dying for. There is nothing that I believe from the bottom of my being.

Nietzsche vents a disturbing thought: We would rather have the void for our purpose than be void of purpose. If there is never anything worth dying for, we tend to will the void, to will destruction. Nihilism. For this gives us, surreptitiously, something to believe in: "There is no belief. There is no reliable knowledge of reality. There is no reliable fullness of being."

James joins Nietzsche in thinking that belief is the *feeling* of reality, and the feeling of our own fullness. They both agree that in losing conventional religious belief, we are left flailing in limbo. For "new tablets,"— new compelling and commanding ultimate beliefs—have not yet been discovered. Christianity was not all childishness, fear, and resentment, for it gave us something constructive to believe in. Sacrificial love need not always be correlated with self-loathing: it can be what Nietzsche in *Thus Spake Zarathustra* called the "gift giving virtue":

> When the sun, over-full, pours itself into the sea. So that even the poorest fisherman rows with golden oars.

Nietzsche thinks that we are afraid to reflect because we suspect what we might find: That we don't really know what we're doing; that we don't have good reasons for what we're doing; that we're not building solid, deep selves; that we don't find that which commands total belief and total commitment and direction. Or that, when some claim to find it, it's fanaticism.

When Nietzsche encourages us "to shoot out a shining star," he is as much cheerleader as sober guide. Not yet himself a member of the new community that must come about if nihilism is to be avoided, he cannot decisively distinguish the shooting out of a star that achieves depth and vitality of self from shooting out a star disintegratively and wildly. Nietzsche foresees many of us today: our countless addictions, distractions, dissipations of passion that might have served as the core of self. Seeking that which we can avow, we find Disney World, or much worse. We do not find objects and ends worthy of our depth and passion. We are led to evasions, and to the silent desperation of which Thoreau spoke, and from which Emerson tried to steer us clear.

Nietzsche had read too much of Schopenhauer to think we moderns could easily locate ourselves and map our course (he had also read Emerson). Opening the door for Nietzsche, Sigmund Freud, and others, Schopenhauer disclosed how we overestimate the powers of self-consciousness. We think we direct our will toward this or that objective, and that we rationally calculate the consequences of achieving it. All the while, vast tides of will are moving us in ways we don't imagine. We are moved inexorably toward many things that give no lasting satisfaction, but which we cannot stop craving.

Most wish to believe that we emerge from our animal pasts. However, our heads chock full of ideas and ideals, we remain in our animal pasts. But not living simply, as do the other animals, we are entangled and confused. We can't come to terms with the will of the species embodied in each of us: the brute will to survive. For Schopenhauer, the willing self is inexplicable, at least in the clear cut sense of mechanistic physicists' "explanation." Following and developing Kant, Schopenhauer believes that this sense of explanation can only be in terms of causal connections discerned between objects.

But our own willing-feeling self cannot be an object for us! We are far too close, too engulfed in it. I the willer *am* my willing. With respect to our own willing-feeling self, all the facile distinctions analytic thinkers draw are out the window: self/other, knower/known, subject/object, emotive/cognitive, willer/willing. And the realization lands with a thud: this willing exceeds the scope of my consciousness, and hence the scope of my cognition, narrowly pinned down and defined.[3]

I *am* this willing-feeling! To gain any grasp on it at all, I—I-myself—must feel the force and pinch of it. One either has the grit and the equanimity to stand open to one's "empirical character" as a particular human animal, or one does not. The self can be sensed only emotively—and morally—and expanded upon only metaphysically, as Schopenhauer does.

Analytic thinkers tend to constrict what intelligence and cognition can mean. But this is insufficient for self-knowledge. To allow one's feeling-willing self to be accessible to some extent, is a moral virtue akin to courage, patience, and, in a sense, love—self-love *and* love of others. (Because for good or ill we do affect others. Are we blessings or afflictions?) The analytic tendency to divide the emotive from the cognitive, and the moral from the factual, is disastrous. In addition to one's own self, some other things can only be known lovingly and resolutely—Jane Goodall's chimpanzees, for but one example.

The endemic weakness of analytic philosophy is just what one should expect: a proneness to making overly simple and rigid distinctions. This, rather than realizing with Nietzsche, Peirce, and James, for instance, that every distinction we draw is good for so much and not a bit more. And that we must be prepared to erase distinctions, and, looking around afresh, make new ones. (What, for example, are the conditions of identity of a supposed "mental state"—"a belief," say—in contrast to a "physical state"?)

At least one more overly facile analytic cut must be pointed out: the "scientific," "cognitive," and "factual," on the one hand, and the "aesthetic" on the other. In many analytic departments of philosophy, aesthetics is not meat and potatoes, but only dessert. But achieving any perspective at all on our feeling-willing lives and selves, is not only a moral and characterological matter; it is an aesthetic one. The moral/aesthetic distinction must be greatly softened.

To disengulf ourselves even partially from the immediate involvements of our subjectivity, James the thinker and artist advises us "to pump free air around things." That is, to gain a certain deliciously delicate and difficult-to-define distance on the true givens of life. We may be able to *say* about something only *that* it is, not *what* it is. Art-making and art-loving can supply this free air, this measure of accessibility of oneself to oneself, this partial deliverance from the otherwise overwhelming grip of impulse and will. Schopenhauer sees this, as does John Dewey. Like Socrates did when, at the end of his life and in a vision, a Presence told him to learn to play a musical instrument.

Do you think the young men in the elevator will ever come to grips with these issues?

Socrates thought the most important learning is remembering matters that we already know, in a sense, but cannot thematize and use effectively in living and thinking. Myth and ritual keep alive this vibrant stratum of our evolved being. They are the funded sensitivity, engagement, perceptiveness, knowledge of the human race, and they must be perpetually revived and revisited.

David Abram writes,

> Our bodies have formed themselves in delicate reciprocity with the manifold textures, sounds, and shapes of an animate earth—our eyes have evolved in subtle interaction with other eyes, as our ears are attuned by their very structure to the howling of wolves and honking of geese.

But Abram goes on,

> I found myself now observing the heron from outside its world, noting with interest its careful, high stepping walk and the sudden dart of its beak into the water, but no longer feeling its tensed yet poised alertness with my own muscles.[4]

When this detachment from the kindred world in which we have evolved and taken shape is crude, automatic, and endemic in a culture, there is vast trouble. In losing resonance, our very being begins to dissipate. We are basically involved, evaluating, passionate beings. As I said, nihilism mangles our roots. What Ingmar Bergman writes of modern art can equally be said of contemporary analytic and "scientific" philosophy at its worst: it is

> free, shameless, irresponsible: the movement is intense, almost feverish, it resembles . . . a snakeskin full of ants. The snake is long since dead, eaten out from within, deprived of its poison, but the skin moves, filled with meddlesome life.[5]

As mentioned, the vast majority of analytic philosophers turn a blind eye to the history of their thought. They cannot understand how the passion with which they have pursued their project of knowing the truth has constricted that project and limited what they can find. Analytic philosophy wants to valorize itself by charting what it takes to be its ever closer convergence with the latest scientific findings (and to develop a metaphysics in the closest possible association with formal logics). Nevertheless, we must at least note some high points in the development of this habit of thought if we would begin to grasp its great limitations.

I mentioned in passing the philosopher-scientists of the seventeenth century. It is particularly Descartes who is germinal in the growth of analytic philosophy through the centuries. In addition to being a mechanistic physicist of a certain bent, he was a mathematician and geometrician of note, and an ambitious physiologist and anatomist. He was not well versed in the history of philosophy. He did pick up the idea of "substance": roughly, that which exists more or less on its own, or in and through itself. He was unaware apparently of the immense subtleties poured into this idea by Aristotle, for example, two thousand years earlier. (And apparently unaware of the Latin mistranslation of *ousia* [the first of the categories for grasping the reality of something] as *substantia*.)

Aristotle would never have thought that a single characteristic of anything, such as some feature that falls in the categories of quantity or location, could adequately demarcate or characterize the being or reality of that thing. But impatient to unroll his scientifically informed world-view, Descartes does think so. There are basically two sorts of substances: Matter, characterized by the key characteristic of being extended (and localized), and mind, characterized by the key characteristic, nonextended (and nonlocalized).

Now, where does Descartes stand when he stakes out his initial philosophical position? What all is he assuming? It is not clear. The question is not really raised and considered, despite his protestations that he wants a self-illuminating and self-authorizing beginning for his thinking. He simply assumes that each thinker is a nonextended, thinking substance. Mind is a nonextended substance that stands by itself. And it reflects itself within itself. Its "contents"—ideas, sensations, mental images—are illuminated within it. In other words, mind is something like a self-illuminating, mirror-lined container (except it is somehow spaceless and without any definite location).

Which leads him, he thinks, to an absolutely certain, self-certifying beginning for his world-view, the famous *cogito ergo sum*. Briefly: Even if a doubt occurs, and then doubt about the doubting, still it must be doubting that is going on "in the mind." And since, he believes, there could not be a doubt or a doubting without a doubter, a thinker, we can be sure of at least one, certain, "originative" truth: I must exist as a thinking thing.

And do I also have a body? That can be doubted!

Now, all this is blatantly counterintuitive. The whole Cartesian approach is eminently doubtable. So far is it from being true that "mind" is essentially self-reflexive, its "contents" self-illuminating! Anyone with any self-awareness knows that thoughts and impulses flit through the margins of consciousness that we are lucky to register at all. Moreover, they never are found alone, as discrete mental contents or elements, but always in a whole flowing experiencing-experienced context, which is the presence in some way of the world around us. Our moment-by-moment life is pre-reflective: we are immediately involved in what presents itself as a whole world, even though most of it is blurred at any particular moment. If we are sane, we feel this world's sustaining, resisting, or affording presence every instant. Sequestering ourselves, prompting ourselves into a crude reflective attitude, we may imagine that we can doubt the "external world's" reality, but we can't really. Not for more than a few moments at least, not without going insane.

The great nineteenth-century American philosopher, Charles Peirce, believed that philosophy's first business is to repudiate Descartes. Here is a key way to locate or site analytic philosophy and to clarify it: A graduate student in some of the "best" universities today can be minted Ph.D. (*doctor philosophicus*) without ever hearing Peirce's name. Though the student may at least hear the names of two thinkers this genius influenced: William James and John Dewey (but recall the Princetonian would never *read* James). All these "pragmatists" agree that Descartes gave a fatefully wrong direction to modern analytic philosophy; he substituted an abstraction and an analysis for a description of what immediately presents itself concretely in living. Thinking that there are discrete mental contents or elements results from an initial reflection and analysis that forgets itself. It smuggles itself in and falls asleep. Mental contents—or so-called "sense data"—are not the building blocks of our minding life, the pragmatists maintained. Rather, they are the by-products, the artifacts, of the analysis that forgets itself.

The pragmatists maintain the primacy of *description:* the description of what actually presents itself in our immediate experiencing (see Essay 4, "Phenomenology in the United States"). The description is of something holistic and encompassing—with a vengeance. In refusing to substitute abstractions and unwitting reflective analysis for descriptions of what is presented concretely and immediately as a surrounding and sustaining presence, in refusing this, pragmatists are also phenomenologists. Thus Peirce can say both that the repudiation of Descartes is the first business of philosophy and that phenomenology is. The two come to the same thing.

And here is another key way of siting, locating, clarifying analytic philosophy: newly minted Ph.D.'s from most of the "best" graduate programs will know nothing about phenomenology. For some reason unknown to them, it will be a thirteen-letter dirty word. They will have no idea of why Hegel's first big book, his voyage of discovery, was a phenomenology, nor of why Peirce (and James and Dewey in their ways) thought that the first business of philosophy is phenomenology. Nor, of course, why Peirce found his categories—his basic ways of sorting out and constituting the experienced world—only within his phenomenology. This stands in sharp contrast to Descartes and his incredibly thin and unfounded categories for "substances"—ones characterized by a single feature, nonextended or extended.

Here is another earmark of analytic philosophy, intimately related to the above: Newly minted Ph.D.'s from many of "the best" graduate programs can be found who know very little of the pivotal figure in modern philosophy, Immanuel Kant.[6] (As Aristotle is the pivotal figure in what professors of philosophy commonly call ancient philosophy.) Kant's philosophy is a protracted and titanic attempt to sew the immediately lived world back together after Descartes chopped it up.

Kant presents his own phenomenology (inadequate though it may be). Before any talk of mental "contents" or "sense data" can be allowed, we must lay out the framework, the context or matrix, without which no discrimination of any particular anythings—"mental" or "physical"—can occur. Ineluctably, as "forms of all possible perception or intuition," we must experience space and time as all-encompassing and continuous wholes. And this before any concepts, even, can be applied to our sense experience. Concepts have instances, Kant says, space has parts.

Analytic philosophy carries the living, unreflected residuum of Descartes's "substantialism, "atomism," "mentalism," his whole glittering trove of reified abstractions and hypostatized nouns for mental "contents"—sensations, images, and such. We get one version or another of what has come to be called phenomenalism. We don't get phenomenology.

Bear with me a bit longer in this all too brief but necessary review of the history of analytic philosophy. We must mention how John Locke fell into line with key features of Descartes's mind/matter dualism. Despite major differences between the two thinkers (prompting writers of histories of philosophy to classify Descartes as a rationalist and Locke as an empiricist), despite this, the latter accepts uncritically Descartes's premature and unfounded analysis of immediate experiencing into mental "entities," "states," "data." At this key point, Locke falls into the cleaving course, the wake, of the "father of modern philosophy."

But it is not until David Hume, emerging well over a century after Descartes, that the pulverizing, detaching, and corrosive—that is, nihilistic—effects of Descartes's thought become fully apparent. Descartes could, it seems, make himself believe that the Christian God exists. So, this creating and sustaining Deity would not have produced beings whose best thought—mechanistic physics, logic, mathematics, and philosophy— would leave them in doubt about the existence of the "external world" and their own bodies! So, Descartes concludes, those doubts can be dismissed.

But with David Hume, all the reassurances of Christianity pretty well dissolve in an acid bath of acute, if constricted, criticism. Accepting Descartes's assumption that the basic resources of thought are discrete mental bits or "contents" in private minds, but rejecting his theological arguments, Hume advances an eerie skepticism. All we can be sure of are sequences of sensations or mental images, vivid or faded, that we take to be appearances of what is happening in the world. But it might not be really happening out there at all. What we take to be one thing causing another may be no more than habits of thinking and expectation we've developed, habits of assembling discrete mental data, habits that might explode the next moment in the face of the unexpected.

And why should Descartes be sure that there must be a continuous self or thinker that has or thinks all these mental contents? Who am I, really? No one can tell. All we can be nearly sure of are the sequences of mental data so far experienced that we just blindly assume to be occurring in a continuous thinking self.

But for all of Hume's critical acuteness, he doesn't question Descartes's basic substantialist and dualist assumptions, his divisions of mind from matter and subjects from objects. Only on these assumptions does Hume's eerie skepticism follow. Analytic philosophy to this day tries to deal with the spectre of Hume. Most analytic philosophers that I've encountered are ignorant of Descartes's great successor and arch-critic, Benedict Spinoza. He judged Descartes to be a confused thinker. The diremption or bifurcation of substances into extended and nonextended is groundless, Spinoza believes. There is only one truly self-standing substance, and everything leans on, is related to, everything else within the one substance. Indeed, there is only one true individual, and it is Nature. Nature or God. And here despite all his geometrical reasoning, Spinoza returns to the mythic roots of Nature religion found in the earliest reaches of human evolution, East or West, North or South.

Carrying heavy remnants of Cartesian thinking, analytic philosophers are practically obsessed with the problem of "reference." How can we be sure that there is anything "out there," and that we can know what it is? Propagated in their thinking is a miasmic feeling of unreality, detachment, uncertainty that can't help but shroud their everyday living in some nebulous way. All the resources of modern modal and nonmodal logics are wedded to a kind of metaphysics in which a referent is rigidly designated "in all possible worlds." (Saul Kripke's notion of naming is a special case in analytic philosophy, and much more in touch with our actual existence. But I cannot deal with it and with him here.)

A corollary: most analytic philosophers will not study our own American critics of Descartes already mentioned. For they must dimly perceive in them a threat to their own basic assumptions. Peirce speaks of "paper doubts": we can pretend to doubt what we can't really, for doubt is not some mental "content in one's mind," but a way of responding and acting in a world we cannot wholly doubt. James responds to "the referent problem" in his typical phenomenological and disarming way. If I grab you by the wrist, we simply cannot doubt—not really—that that place on your body where I feel you is exactly where you feel yourself felt. We "refer" to the very same place.

Except, of course, it is not "reference" at all, but the practical certainty of immediate involvement in an essentially interrelated world. It is an existential certainty without which sanity would be impossible.

Analytic philosophy tends powerfully to put us at a remove from everything, even from our own selves, selves turned ghostly. As if the self were a kind of theatre in which we sit and try to identify ourselves on a stage—try to identify ourselves out there as objects (recall Schopenhauer's critique of construals of self-knowledge in subject/object terms). Not finding ourselves out there, we may conclude that we can't really find ourselves at all. Or, it's as if, in a delusional sweat, we ran outside our house, looked back in through a window, and were surprised that we couldn't see ourselves in there.

Yet again, perhaps the whole Cartesian world-view can be compared to those large plastic cubicles, found in some diners and amusement parks. The bottom of the cubicle is loaded with goodies: toy cars, glittering zircon bracelets, strings of beads, packs of cigarettes, puppets, chocolates sheathed in foil to look like outsized silver dollars. Above them all is poised a magnificent claw. After putting coins in slots, you can manipulate the claw downwards and clamp its jaws shut on just the thing you want in the jumble and tangle of treasures. And perhaps you will fail and get the wrong thing, or get nothing.

Whatever its drawbacks and virtues as academic philosophy (I of course am emphasizing its drawbacks), judged on a psychoanalytic as well as an existential level analytic philosophy may well be the ultimate defense mechanism. The mechanism employed by those who feel dimly but profoundly their vulnerability as body-selves—what I mentioned in the preface. Descartes thought that humans are composite beings, half mental, half physical. Animals are only physical beings, and mechanical ones at that. So when an animal is vivisected and shrieks, it may sound like it is feeling pain, but it is really no more than a machine that shrieks because it is blocked in its functioning, or because it is unlubricated. It is hard to imagine any presumptively sane view more out of touch with reality.

Though some analytic thinkers may repudiate Descartes's precise formulations, most keep the endemic detachment and schizy unreality that goes with the Cartesian territory. Thus there is little analytic work on the primal stages of human evolution, studies of the mythic and ritualistic grounds of human existence. Work on "the environment" and on "environmental ethics" does occur, but tends as expected to be thin and detached, with many reified abstractions, "rights," "duties," and so on.

But we are not only *in* environments, as marbles are in a box. We are of them, constituted fully or scantily of their being. Detachment kills immediacy of involvement, and its sustenance and sap. Kills our kinship with plants and animals, and our ecstatic oneness with sky, mountain, sun, wind, bird, and native peoples. Insofar as this is the case, analytic philosophy is nihilistic.

Here's a trichotomy that may orient us. First, there's the domain of what we know and know that we know; second, the domain of what we know we don't know; third, the domain of what we don't know we don't know. The latter is, of course, unplumbable, undemarcatable. We simply sense, dumbly discern, that we are engulfed in an encompassing reality that cannot itself be encompassed or circumscribed.

I understand philosophy in a traditional way. It is an activity the ultimate aim of which is to keep us open to the unencompassable, the domain of what we don't know we don't know. An obvious corollary is to strive to make our assumptions as clear and as grounded in experience as it is possible for us to make them. For our assumptions are just that: assumptions, which we formulate within a universe we cannot encompass in thought. Analytic philosophy tends to so sharply focus that it seals us from the vague but all-important background presence of the universe. It feeds a starvation diet to us strange thinking animals. It is crudely or subtly nihilistic.

Assumptions made automatically very often pinch off in advance the full sustaining and regenerating flow of the universe through us, through our resonating bodies and nervous and glandular systems. This is certainly true of Descartes, all his strained arguments for the existence of God to the contrary not withstanding. It remains true of the analytic tradition, at least the main channel of it. Truth, for example, in this channel is typically construed as a correspondence between propositions "in the mind" and the world "out there." But these are all reified abstractions, not the flowing life of involvement in whole surrounds that we bodily beings actually live.

And think of it! Why should truth be restricted to *words?* All the unencompassable ways the world is revealed to us constitute truth. Silences, music, gestures, presences and presencings here and there. Animals, birds, trees, indigenous peoples, all these beings can be true when they are true to themselves, true to their nature, and their nature is shown us.

Our own American pragmatist-phenomenologists converge not only with the earliest thought in European or Western philosophy, but also (as I have recently argued in a book) with indigenous thought worldwide.[7] They tune in to the primal level of experience. They set us free in the presence of the universe. It's not as if this current of American thought had simply been replaced by analytic concerns. John Dewey died in 1952. Henry Bugbee—author of *The Inward Morning*—died at Christmas, 1999. They, and others, kept writing and teaching. Bugbee recalls us to fullness of presence and of truth:

> As true stillness comes upon us, we hear, we hear, and we learn that our whole lives may have the character of finding that anthem which would be native to our own tongue, and which alone can be the true answer for each of us to the questioning, the calling, the demand for ultimate reckoning which devolves upon us.[8]

It's not as if such voices were not raised, voices of hearkening and reckoning. The analytic tide simply drowned them out in many university philosophy departments.

I seem to hear William James asking for clarification of "tide" in "analytic tide." He demands we spell out its consequences for our experience, "cash it." Immediately we are turned again to face the unencompassable encompassing. No more than with "the universe" can we pin down and isolate the meaning of "analytic tide." We sense viscerally the unplumbable domain of what we don't know we don't know. Why has the tide arisen, what are its limits, just where will it flow, and will it subside? Our ability to know what moves us individually and corporately is greatly limited—unimaginably limited.

Not to acknowledge this is to be sucked further into nihilism, vain thrashing around and zombie-like unreality. No doubt, my own attempt to link analytic habits of thought and nihilism is more limited and flawed than I can imagine. But, of course, I do believe I should try. I easily concede that there are more subtleties and borderline cases of analytic thought than I have acknowledged. Yet, there is an analytic habit of mind that tends to pinch down the fullness of experiencing, to weaken the force of its flow. Inevitably, the analytic habit diminishes the fullness, weight, and sustaining presence of the world experienced by us, and the fullness, weight, and sustaining presence of our own experiencing selves.

Pause a moment with works that I believe can be called analytic and that exhibit this deracinating tendency, Douglas Husak's *Drugs and Rights* (New York and Cambridge, England, 1992), and several of Thomas Nagel's works. (Nobody will charge me with picking on weaklings.)

Husak defends with great apparent clarity and logical rigor the view that the recreational use of psychoactive drugs should be legalized. One can learn much from the book. Nevertheless, it is clear to me that Husak's horizon has shrunk, and probably before he knew it. Any vision unencumbered by analytic methodological focusing and strictures would see that the probability of addiction for some of those who use drugs recreationally is not insignificant. But nowhere in the book does the phenomenon of addiction show itself in its fullness and violence. Any unencumbered survey of the subject matter, any disciplined looking around, any phenomenology, would have shown how disastrous addiction can be for some people. It destroys their own and often their family's lives. Husak contents himself with exploding the common view that "drug addicts cannot stop." Because some do, and some of these stop "cold turkey."

But the palpable fact is that many try to stop and cannot, and their own lives and their relatives' are gravely impaired or destroyed. And note a limitation of view that I find remarkable in Husak, a philosopher of law: even though it may be that only a minority of those who use drugs recreationally get addicted, doesn't our whole system of laws aim, among other things, to protect the minority? Don't we try to protect people from their reckless urges? Don't we, for example, try to protect people from bashing their brains out riding motorcycles by requiring them to wear a helmet?

Now turn to the well-known contemporary philosopher Thomas Nagel. Some may think that he's too freewheeling a thinker to be labelled "analytic." I do agree that he is freewheeling, comparatively at least, and certainly very interesting to read. But an analytic tendency limits his vision unnecessarily. Thirty years ago and more I would have predicted a greater growth in his thought than has in fact occurred. For example, that long ago he published a truly creative and liberating article, "Sexual Perversion." (Reprinted in *Mortal Questions,* New York: Cambridge University Press, 1979). It was influenced, to be sure, by Jean-Paul Sartre's mordant phenomenology of interpersonal relations. But Nagel opened out on horizons that Sartre seldom or ever intimates. Nagel exhibits sexual perversion as a short-circuiting of fully regenerative cycles of human interactive sexual activity. It's not just the alluring and arousing "look" of the other, but what the look leads to in time—or doesn't lead to. Does it lead to growth in the world for each party? Though always suitably reserved, cool, professional, Nagel was, I think, opening the way to the deepest reaches of human experience, possibly to grounding myths and rituals of regenerativity that have sustained us immemorially.

I was puzzled and ultimately disappointed by Nagel's more recent *The View from Nowhere* (New York: Oxford University Press, 1986). I had expected the phenomenology evident in the earlier article to be more matured, more active on a broader scale, but no.

First of all, the reader can't help but be impressed by Nagel's persistent and noble attempt to avoid reductionism. His writing reminds me some of Gabriel Marcel's *Homo Viator.* We can at best be said to be on our way to understanding ourselves—or at least to be trying very hard. For there are two apparently irreducible ways to understand things. And since they are ours, we must try to live with them both, but they are largely incompatible. First, "the view from nowhere," That is, the "external standpoint," or what science discovers by systematically ruling out what appears to only one, or a very few, particular points of view; and counting only what can be discovered by any competent inquirers, adequately equipped, at any place or time (and centrally employing the universal language of mathematics).

Second, the view from somewhere, what each of us turns up and lives through in our immediate, first person, "internal" viewpoint. Neither view gives us any ultimate understanding of how reality might be disclosed irrespective of human observation, experience, interpretation.

There is a note of humility here, perhaps of mystery. What a relief to hear such a voice in "the better" departments of philosophy today! However, at the risk of appearing ungrateful, I will make a few critical remarks. I don't mind at all the tragic note in Nagel, but I don't think it's quite on pitch. Moreover, it should be sounded in a larger composition. God knows, reconciliation of viewpoints is difficult enough in this world without Nagel's reading of subjectivity that eccentrically emphasizes the privacy of individual consciousness and viewpoint, and also the gulf that divides the internal viewpoint from the external. Our contemporary feeling of alienation, isolation, abandonment are baneful enough without exacerbating them.

What prevented Nagel's "Sexual Perversion" from moving out decisively into the mytho-cultural historical and prehistorical background that it opened up (for me at least) is still at work in his writing. He inadequately unpacks subjectivity. There is a detectable residue of Cartesian psycho/physical dualism and premature objectification—despite what I imagine will be his protests to the contrary.

This can be seen in his justly famous, "What is it Like to be a Bat?" (*Philosophical Review,* Vol. 82, No. 4, Oct. 1974). In some fundamental ways, Nagel seems to agree with phenomenologists. For a prime example, he implicitly agrees with Husserl's basic critique of Descartes: that he leaves the individual ego as "a tag-end of the world." That is, that Descartes has, unwittingly and automatically, abstracted himself from immediacy of involvement in the encompassing and permeating world. Everything for him is an object of some sort—even a mind is! Inevitably, his thought must go out of touch with his own self. The question is whether Nagel adequately develops this implicit agreement with Husserl.

In his article, "What is it Like to be a Bat?", Nagle rejects both behaviorism and functionalism, for they both prematurely objectify mind and body. He *tries* to rediscover our subjectivity (not subjectivism!): how we are actually living our lives and experiencing the world every moment.

We understand others—insofar as we do so at all—only empathically. As he poses the fundamental question, What's it like for that subject of experience to have that experience? he has us look for analogies that link various subjects' experiencing of some agreed upon thing. "Yes, it hurts like fire when you touch it," or "Right, you feel good after you do it," etc.

Now, what's it like to be a *bat?* Here is a distant species, and empathy is stretched perilously close to the breaking point. Nagel rightly emphasizes that we shouldn't try to imagine our consciousness in the bat's body; this would be more Cartesianism, he says. He probably holds to something like what I call body-self: consciousness is something our bodies do. And note well: he doesn't assert that we have *no* idea of what it's like to be a bat. But he does assert that bats are "a fundamentally *alien* form of life."

At this point, Nagel, again, disappoints me. We find, ironically, a deficiency of empathic feeling: a deficiency in his account of the potentialities and actualities of immediate involvement in the world, his account of our subjectivity. In a much more subtle form than is usual for many philosophers today, we encounter yet again pervasive and endemic modern loneliness, desiccation, alienation. Calvin Martin writes brilliantly,

> One of the great insights of hunter societies is that words and artifice of specific place and place-beings (animal and plant) constitute humanity's primary instruments of self-location . . . for mankind is fundamentally an echo-locator, like our distant relatives the porpoise and the bat . . . Only by learning . . . *true* words and *true* artifice about these things can one hope to become . . . a genuine person . . . To be mendacious about other-than-human persons springs back upon us to make us mendacious about ourselves. (*In the Spirit of the Earth: Rethinking History and Time,* Baltimore: Johns Hopkins University Press, 1992, p. 103)

Even with Nagel, we lose in the end our profound kinship with all beings, particularly living ones. So we lose an essential ingredient of ourselves. This would have greatly disturbed Native Americans, and it should disturb us. To really empathize with other beings we must empathize and resonate with ourselves. We must really unpack our subjectivity. If we do, we will discover that there are specific analogies between our experiencing and a bat's. Though presumably we do not send out sonar pulses, measurable only by sensitive instruments, exactly as do bats, we do send out sounds (to take but this sensory modality). And we do "read" the response to these sounds from the world. This is done usually unconsciously—that is, unacknowledgeably.

We emit slight sighs and groans and holdings of breath and gasps, and rustlings, and fidgetings, and slight laughs of recognition or contempt, and tremors of delight or pain, and so forth. And the response to these from the larger world is immediately registered and molds our ensuing behavior, whether of attraction or avoidance or delay in response. We are echo-locators.

In fact, without supposing that this nearly constant echo-location goes on, I don't believe we can begin to explain the behavior of most analytic philosophers today. I mean their otherwise nearly incredible avoidance of any real encounter with philosophical positions that question analytic preconceptions and dualistic assumptions. Very like bats, they echo-locate or prehend certain things as just "to be avoided" (the quotes lend articulation to the mute response). These things are not further characterized. Or, they are characterized as "not to be further characterized." Though perhaps accompanied by a fidget, or a nearly inaudible snort of contempt. The suppression of otherness is concealed, and the concealment is concealed, at least from everybody in their group—and from very many in the wider philosophical society that they dominate. Cartesian alienation haunts even Nagel.

P. F. Strawson closes his review of *The View from Nowhere* ("Inside/ Outside," *The New Republic,* Oct. 17, 1986):

> Finally, death. . . . Nagel is much possessed . . . by the terrifying thought of annihilation, the expectation of nothingness. Internally it is impossible to see one's death as the incident that, externally, it is.

This is an accurate summation that points up the inadequacy of the Inside/ Outside distinction itself. True, nobody can be experiencing the world exactly as I am, but that is because nobody else can live my body as I do.

But we are fed back through others into ourselves. We are echo-locators. Certain others easily find our deaths significant, and this confirms our own sense of our death's significance. In a real way, they laugh our laughs and cry our cries. A balanced sense of the significance of one's death is found in neither the "internal view" construed tacitly as a Cartesian substance or private theatre, nor in the "external" view from nowhere, which misses our reality and preciousness as persons.

The external view of science can provide only statistics and depersonalizing facts. Both Inside and Outside views presuppose a ground they do not acknowledge. This can only be supplied by a phenomenology in tune with both the reality of persons and the reality of science.

I have reiterated that Cartesianism, and the analytic philosophy that follows in its wake, generates an eerie feeling of detachment and unreality. But the fact of the feeling is real enough, is burden enough, and it is hard to shake! Nothing better reveals the persistence of Cartesian assumptions than the way they hobbled analytic philosophers in the twentieth century who presented themselves as champions of science.

In the 1920s, physicists Werner Heisenberg and Niels Bohr were forced to conclude that observing atomic particles disturbed the entities observed. Just before this time, Bertrand Russell was still distinguishing idealism from realism: the former he characterized as believing that knowing affects the known, the latter—realism, the position Russell favored—characterized as denying that it does. Russell could maintain his position only on the tacit Cartesian assumption that knowing occurs "in the mind," and does not affect "the outer world."[9]

Another example, this time in the 1930s: the hard-nosed "scientific" philosopher and logical positivist, Rudolph Carnap, tried to develop a world-view by using only mental "sense data" (*The Logical Structure of the World,* originally published in 1928, Berlin). He thought of these as immediate observables, "hard data." He wagered on a phenomenalism deeply influenced by Descartes's mental/physical dualism. Not a surveying and staking-out of where thinkers find themselves initially situated—not a phenomenology! And, mind you, this at the very time scientists themselves were being forced by their experiments to discard Cartesian assumptions. This at the time A. N. Whitehead, for example, had developed an organismic cosmology that sedulously dismantled and discarded the Cartesian bifurcation of nature into matter and mind. This at the time science itself was carrying us to the position epitomized fairly recently by John Wheeler, "There's no *out there* out there."[10]

At this very time, "scientific" philosophers calling themselves logical positivists were digging in their heels to slow or prevent the movement. Like Descartes who wrote so seriously on the correct method of investigation, these philosophers were trying to canonize *the* scientific method. Trying to achieve the sure method of success, the sure way to positive knowledge.

There's something pathetically anxiety ridden going on here. While scientists themselves were entertaining the wildest sounding hypotheses to account for their actual observations and experiments, these philosophers were digging in their heels: looking for certainty as had their mentor Descartes centuries earlier [see John Dewey, *The Quest for Certainty*, (New York: Minton, Balch and Co., 1929]. The scientists themselves were moving toward the "super string theory" that appeared eruptively at the end of the twentieth century (as one physicist called it: a theory meant for the twenty-first century that had somehow emerged in the twentieth; see Brian Greene, *The Elegant Universe*, (New York: Vintage Books, 2000).

Super string theory recalls—for anyone who knows the history of philosophy—the work of the pre-Socratic musician-mathematician-scientist, Pythagoras. The idea is that atomic "particles" are really exceedingly short "strings" that resonate in many interlacing musical-like vibratory patterns. This theory holds the possibility at least of synthesizing theories of the very large and those of the very small, a division that has vexed scientists for decades.

The culture lag exhibited by "scientific" analytic philosophers in roughly the past hundred years nearly boggles the mind. Indeed, it will boggle the mind unless we suppose what I have been supposing: that they are encaged within Cartesian dualistic assumptions—encumbered, benumbed—thinking completely uncritically within these assumptions. Never has the truth of George Santayana's famous aphorism been better exhibited: Those who are ignorant of the past are doomed to repeat it. And those ignorant of the deep past tend to be ignorant of the recent past as well.

Thus few analytic philosophers today would call themselves logical positivists. "We're no longer back in the '30s." Yet the deep assumptions persist. For example (and to allude again to what I have mentioned), the positivists, honing their distinctions and reified abstractions, split off the cognitive from the emotive. (As if any perception of anything whatsoever perceived wasn't bathed in at least a minimal evaluational and emotive aura—"important enough to be noticed.")

But the cognitive/emotive split keeps emerging in some form or other. It's like the Hydra: cut off one of its heads and two more grow in its place. For instance, a young philosopher of physics objected to one of my points by saying, "Well, that earlier idea may have *inspired* physicist X, but it doesn't figure in the *content* of his theory." I should have expostulated, "Unpack the concept of inspiration!" But at the time I did not. So easy it is to be sucked into the lagging, sluggish, turbid stream of human intellectual evolution—benumbed in some professional group.

Looking back on the twentieth century is worth the time. At its midpoint, a fateful article appeared from the noted logician-philosopher, Willard Quine: "Two Dogmas of Empiricism" (reprinted in *From a Logical Point of View*, Cambridge, Mass., 1953). Very briefly, for our purposes here, the dogmas consist in believing that a sharp line is to be drawn between synthetic propositions (the predicate cannot be inferred purely conceptually from the subject of the proposition), which are always factual propositions about the way the world happens to be—and which are to be established by scientific-empirical investigation. And, on the other hand, propositions that are necessarily true, but are always analytic: that is to say, the predicate can be inferred purely conceptually or formal-logically from the subject.

Quine was beginning to dismember Cartesian dualism. (Carnap was reported to be deeply disturbed when characterized by Quine as a Cartesian metaphysician.) This dualism regarded necessarily true or analytic truths as completely mind-born. While empirical or synthetic propositions mark the discovery of the "external world," the "pure facts" of what's happening "out there." Quine pointed out the artificiality and nonexhaustiveness of the distinction. What we actually find when we actually look around, Quine says, is a single field of experience of the world in its organic interconnectedness. When investigations of various kinds turn up what is unexpected—anomalies—there are several ways we can accommodate the field of knowledge or experience to them. One is by altering our propositions at the empirical "edges" of the field. Another is by altering propositions that appear to be more "central" or "inner" in the field, that is, propositions linked within themselves more or less purely conceptually. The question of which course to take is to be decided on pragmatic grounds (in some sense): what best works to further investigation? Or what, at least, we think at the time will further it.

Immediately felt is the affinity to the great American pragmatists, their anti-Cartesianism, and their idea of truth as that which effectively leads us and involves us in the world. They saw that there are no purely empirical facts "out there." What we call empirical facts carry a heavy conceptual freight. We pick things out and notice them only within evolving conceptual and valuational networks. Josiah Royce, who called himself an absolute pragmatist, insisted that the very concept of the empirical is not an empirical concept. That is, we can't weigh, measure, or locate the

concept. Empirical research is guided and influenced by all kinds of ide-
ational, evaluative, and existential matters. When Quine began to see what
some were going to do with his article of 1951, he was appalled. He thought
they planned to dethrone science. What a can of worms he had opened!

He took drastic steps. He limited the organically interrelated field of
experience and knowledge to *natural-scientific* knowledge (or to what he
thought is essentially connected to such knowledge). The great pragmatists
of the past would never have done that. As Wotan sequestered Brunhilde
within a circle of sacred fire, so Quine sought to sequester science. He was
aiming at the ultimate encirclement, the ultimate protection of pure "objectivity" against subjectivity and poetry, that he finally projected in his
From Stimulus to Science.

Where do we go from here? Things are not hopeless. One of my
teachers, Sidney Hook, told us a story about his teacher, John Dewey. He
once held up his fountain pen in class and said, "Whenever I pick this up I
become a revolutionary."

Philosophy is created out of a profound human need and urge: to
explore beyond anything already known, or even imagined. This need and
urge cannot be penned up and contained for very long, not by any sacred
fire, not by anything, not even by mimetic engulfment in professional
groups. For example, the very fact that some analytic philosophers are
becoming seriously involved in twentieth and twenty-first century physics
bodes nothing but good, I think. The revolutions in the new physics are
paradigmatically philosophical ones, though the physicists do not pick up
their checks in philosophy departments. The best antidote to logical
positivists' Cartesian rigidities, indeed, all their artificial and strained
dichotomies, is the history of twentieth-century science itself. For instance,
Werner Heisenberg did not think he was merely "emotively" involved—or
getting "inspired"—when he read Plato on the elementary geometric
solids. For it contributed at a certain crucial point to his *cognition* of the
world.[11]

No, things are not hopeless. Phenomenology cannot be suppressed
forever. Nor can it be mindlessly confused with phenomenalism forever.
Already, informed people are seeing that phenomenology and science work
hand in hand.[12] As we need disciplined and distinctive ways to observe
different subject-matters (for example, specimens of organic molecules
under a microscope, or feasible routes up a mountain we plan to climb), so

we need a disciplined way to observe and describe consciousness. Analytic philosophers' haphazard "intuitions" are laughably inadequate.

Contra Descartes, consciousness is not a self-illuminating chamber that holds self-evident mental entities. Primal human awareness overlaps with that of other animals. Primal awareness is pre-reflective, it is "scious-ness," as James said, not *con*sciousness, not awareness of awareness. It is the immediate sensing and perceiving of a sensed and perceived in the world. It is "double barreled," as James and Dewey saw. We should never use single-barreled terms like experience, or percept, or sense-datum. But rather, experiencing of an experienced, or perceiving of a perceived, or sensing of something sensed. (Or as Edmund Husserl put it, coupled indissolubly together is the act of awareness and its intentional object.)[13]

Only when we make these elementary distinctions is there any hope of using our descriptions of consciousness to suggest hypotheses about "underlying" brain functioning (note the scare quotes). These hypotheses can then be checked against ever-improving PET scans of the brain. Heightened discipline has numerous advantages. We will be as suspicious of the sclerotic hypostatization "brain states" as we will be of "mental states." We will know to ask, for example, How accurate and how comprehensive are the pictures delivered on our currently available PET scanners?

Or, as the physicist Roger Penrose has asked, Might the ultimate units of brain functioning be not the individual neurons, but the microtubules of these which generate webs of quantum influence, perhaps superposition, through the brain (and beyond?). This would have to be understood in terms of a quantum physics not yet fully grasped.

No, things are not hopeless at all. Persistence and hopefulness are everything.

Notes

1. I opened the Leiter Gourmet Report (2000–2001) and saw at once two statements purporting to be factual that are glaringly false. In an attempt to defend his report in the face of mounting criticism, Brian Leiter maintains that *all* [emphasis his] state university philosophy graduate departments "self-define" as "analytic." From where I sit in central New Jersey, not quite two hundred miles to the west is Penn State, and about one hundred miles to the east is SUNY Stony Brook. These state universities boast large and healthy graduate programs that are

obviously pluralistic. No member of either department would self-define their group as analytic. I think Leiter's selective inattention can best be explained as typical of a clique, a cult, a coterie (though one that may be slowly dissolving). Sigmund Freud writes,

> A group is extraordinarily credulous and open to influence, it has no critical faculty, and the improbable does not exist for it. It thinks in images, which call one another up by association . . . and whose agreement with reality is never checked by any reasonable agency. The feelings of a group are always very simple and very exaggerated. So that a group knows neither doubt nor uncertainty. . . . Inclined as it itself is to all extremes, a group can only be excited by excessive stimulus. Anyone who wishes to produce an effect upon it needs no logical adjustment in his arguments; he must paint in the most forcible colors, he must exaggerate, and he must repeat the same thing again and again. (*Group Psychology and Analysis of the Ego*, J. Strachey, trans., New York: W. W. Norton, 1959 [1922], p. 10)

Caught up in a tempest in a teapot, participants lose all sense of the teapot. Self-interested journalists and the mass media get caught up as well. Note, for example, the newspaper of record, the *New York Times* (Dinitra Smith, "New York is Home to Bright Lights and Big Thinkers", 3 February 2001). The reporter follows Leiter's lead, as do many students, administrators, and some professors seeking guidance or status. When professors of *philosophy* get caught up in their mass-media image as "Big Thinkers," the result is hilarious—gamey, marvelous, tragic farce.

2. There has finally appeared a thorough critical history of analytic philosophy: Nicholas Capaldi, *The Enlightenment Project in the Analytic Conversation* (Dordrecht and Boston: Kluwer Publishers, 1998). Capaldi is uniquely qualified to produce it, having written a dissertation at Columbia on Hume years ago, and articles on Enlightenment figures since then, as well has having been active in the Pluralist movement in the APA (see Essay 3). His is an extremely important book, a publishing event. It will no longer be easy for analytic philosophers to assume that theirs is a kind of *philosophia perennis*. That is, they believe that analytic philosophy is the funding of all that is worth preserving in previous philosophy: the essence of the right method and the right results that will recur from year to year. It doesn't need a history.

Anyone attentive to the analytic scene, and not just caught up in it, will wonder how thinkers classified as philosophers could find themselves so isolated in the culture, so parochial. As has Capaldi, John McCumber adds a revealing piece to the picture-puzzle. His contribution is more restricted, but it is added at a point in the gestalt that brings out a deep wrinkle never before revealed, I think. Note well his *Time in a Ditch: American Philosophy in the McCarthy Era* (Evanston, IL: Northwestern University Press, 2001). This book throws a bright light on one of the motivations for some of those philosophers who tried to appear scientific. If they appeared that way, they hoped to appear non-ideological, and if they appeared to be that, how could they appear to be communists or communist sympathizers? Both Capaldi's and McCumber's contributions are publishing events gratefully acknowledged.

3. Arthur Schopenhauer, *On the Fourfold Root of the Principle of Sufficient Reason* trans. by F. F. J. Payne (LaSalle, IL: Open Court, 1974 [1813, revised ed. 1847], intro. by Richard Taylor, particularly pp. 210–216.) Schopenhauer, anticipating Freud, illuminates the elusiveness and befuddling opacity of the self as simultaneously and identically willer *and* willing.

> The influence which the will exercises on knowledge is based not on causality proper, but on the identity . . . of the knowing with the willing subject . . . the will's activity is so direct that we often are not clearly conscious thereof. It is so rapid that at times we are not even conscious of the occasion for a representation that is thus brought about. Here it seems as though something quite unconnected with anything else has entered our consciousness. That this, however, cannot occur, is . . . precisely the root of the principle of sufficient reason . . . Every picture or image that is suddenly presented to our imagination, also every judgment that does not follow its previously existing ground or reason, must be produced by an act of will which has a motive, although such motive is often not perceived because it [seems] insignificant, and the act of will is frequently not noticed because its fulfillment is so easy that this and the wish are simultaneous.

Most impressive!

4. David Abram, "The Ecology of Magic," *Orion* (Summer 1991), pp. 38–39. See also his *The Spell of the Sensuous* (New York: Pantheon, 1996). These are delightfully readable and important existential-phenomenological investigations.

5. Quoted in Paisley Livingston, *Ingmar Bergman and the Rituals of Art* (Ithaca and London: Cornell University Press, 1982), p. 14. I thank Harry Redner for this reference. The passage is requoted in my *Wild Hunger: The Primal Roots of Modern Addiction* (Lanham, MD and London: Rowman and Littlefield, 1998), p. 188.

6. True, some philosophers commonly accounted for as "analytic" have done some excellent work on portions of Kant's corpus of writings. I think of

Wilfrid Sellars and P. F. Strawson. In particular, I think of two of the latter's books, *Individuals: An Essay in Descriptive Metaphysics* and *The Bounds of Sense*. But neither Sellars nor Strawson, I think, grasps adequately the world-historical—the pivotal—significance of Kant for the history of philosophy, and for human history in general. The analytic tendency to break down topics and issues into manageable pieces restricts their view. Kant's whole development over the decades of his adult life, from Newtonian astrophysicist to exploratory metaphysician, is not seen (or if glimpsed, not properly emphasized). Hence the great philosophers of the nineteenth century who followed him—and who tried to round out his views, so to speak—are typically passed over in "the better" graduate programs (I mean Fichte, Schelling, Hegel, Schopenhauer, Marx, Feurbach, Stirner, Peirce, James, Royce, Dewey, and others). Kant is a hugely seminal thinker. Press on him at one point and get positivism. At another, pragmatism, and/or some version of phenomenology. At still another closely related point, various versions of existentialism, e.g., religious existentialism. Most graduate students in "the better" departments have no idea of all this, hence have no idea of where we're all coming from, whether we know it or not. For example, they do not see Kant's uncritical incorporation of the Cartesian (and the British empiricists') unwitting and premature analysis of primal sensuousness into a series of discrete mental entities or states. So they cannot distinguish phenomenalism from phenomenology, and cannot appreciate pragmatists' and phenomenologists' descriptions of the integrity of our primal emotional, volitional, and intellectual lives—what must be understood holistically. Insofarforth, these students and their professors contribute to nihilism.

7. Bruce Wilshire, *The Primal Roots of American Philosophy: Pragmatism, Phenomenology, and Native American Thought,* Univ. Park: Penn State Univ. Press, 2000.

8. Henry Bugbee, *The Inward Morning: A Philosophical Exploration in Journal Form* (Athens, GA: University of Georgia Press, 4th printing 1999, [1958]).

9. Using Bertrand Russell as a paradigmatic case, one can learn about analytic philosophy and its wordless assumptions—what I call its assumed detachment, its initial posit of the world as the total collection of objects or topics. This learning would be particularly informative if Russell were contrasted with an acquaintance of his in the teens of the last century, D. H. Lawrence. See Dolores LaChapelle, *D. H. Lawrence: Future Primitive* (Denton: University of North Texas Press, 1996), especially Chapter 4, "Mind and Nature." Lawrence's denunciations of Russell (in a letter to him, for example, "It is *not* hatred of falsehood which inspires you. It is hatred of people, of flesh and blood"), these denunciations should not be laid to extreme personal and temperamental differences only. They indicate also utterly fundamental philosophical disagreements about the nature of

knowledge and reality—fundamentally different world-posits. Along with James, Dewey, and Heidegger, Lawrence does not sunder the cognitive from the emotive. For example, what Dewey means by the necessity of a prior apprehension of the qualia of a whole situation of inquiry, and what Heidegger means by the cognitive power of mood (or *Befindlichkeit*), Lawrence attempts to capture in his novels as the total drift and pull of a place and time. (For instance, see his *The Plumed Serpent*, N.Y.: Vintage Books, 1992 [1926], pp. 68–76. Here he describes the encompassing situation in a devastated Mexico following the revolution as "pulling you down, down.")

10. Cited in Tor Norretranders, *The User Illusion: Cutting Consciousness Down to Size* trans. by J. Suydenham (New York: Viking, 1998 [1991]), p. 201.

11. Werner Heisenberg, *Physics and Beyond: Encounters and Conversations* (New York: Harper Torchbooks, 1971), pp. 237ff. Articles from 1919 to 1965 trans. by A. J. Pomerans.

12. See, for example, Bruce Mangan, "Taking Phenomenology Seriously," *Consciousness and Cognition* 2 (1993), pp. 89–108; Shaun Gallagher, "Mutual Enlightenment: Recent Phenomenology in Cognitive Science," *Journal of Consciousness Studies* 4, 3 (1997), especially p. 210; finally, Roger Penrose, *Shadows of the Mind: A Search for the Missing Science of Consciousness*, New York and Oxford: Oxford Univ. Press, 1994.)

13. Thinkers who use single-barreled terms such as "percept" are phenomenalists in the grip of Cartesianism (a percept is "something in the mind"). They do not understand what phenomenologists mean by intentional object, or thing-as-perceived (through or in some perceiving). They probably think that phenomenologists are naive realists who cannot account for error. But phenomenologists do not simply equate thing-as-perceived and thing. Given the immense complexity of the circulation of energies involving thing-there-needing-to-be-perceived and organism-as-perceiver, all kinds of matters can go wrong in the transaction, the interchange! The thing-as-perceived need not be isomorphic with the thing-there-needing-to-be-perceived (we may mistake a wild animal for a bush rustling in the twilight). And this delusion may be attributable to the *perceiving* at that time and place being untowardly influenced by soporific drugs, say. But when we are perceiving veridically, there must be some considerable overlap between thing as intentional object, thing-as-perceived, and thing-there-needing-to-be-perceived. (And there must be some minimal overlap when we are perceiving nonveridically, otherwise nobody could ever discover what we were mistaken about.)

2

"The Ph.D. Octopus":
William James's Prophetic Grasp of the
Failures of Academic Professionalism

Nearly one hundred years ago, William James was ahead of most of us. In "The Ph.D. Octopus" (1903) he foresaw the existential crisis into which the professionalization of disciplines and the segmentation and bureaucratization of the university were leading us.

> America is . . . rapidly drifting towards a state of things in which no man of science or letters will be accounted respectable unless some kind of badge or diploma is stamped upon him, and in which bare personality will be a mark of outcast estate. It seems to me high time to rouse ourselves to consciousness, and to cast a critical eye upon this decidedly grotesque tendency. Other nations suffer terribly from the Mandarin disease. Are we doomed to suffer like the rest?[1]

What happens to our sense of ourselves—our cemented sense of our significance and worth—when to establish our identity we must display certificates stamped by institutions? Particularly by ones to which we have never wholeheartedly bonded? James fears that our identity will crumble, in spite of all the shiny facades erected around it.

James's voice intermixes with other prophetic ones: Kierkegaard's— that lampooning of learned professors who build a mansion of world-historical thought but live in a shack out back; Nietzsche's (quoted in my preface)[2]—

> The proficiency of our finest scholars, their heedless industry, their heads smoking day and night, their very craftsmanship: how often the real meaning of all this lies in the desire to keep something hidden from oneself!

Dostoevsky's—

> Ah . . . nowadays everything's all mixed up . . . we don't have any especially
> sacred traditions in our educated society; it's as if somebody patched some-
> thing together the best he could out of books . . . or extracted it out of the
> ancient chronicles. But those would be the scholars, and they're all block-
> heads . . .

And we can't leave Dostoevsky without hearing the spiteful voice of the
Underground Man who complains of his inability to become, to *be*,
anything—even an insect.

Finally let us hear for a moment that balked and despairing but
persevering giant, Max Weber, who details in *Economy and Society* "the
iron cage of bureaucracy."[3]

What is it that all these voices lament? It's simply stated but difficult
to unpack the meaning: To be we must be validated by the universe that
evolved us and holds us. When our place within the universe is no longer
guaranteed by ages-old religions and their rituals, or by settled modes of
principled ethical thought, the vacuum draws into itself untested institutions, turned obsessively within themselves, to stamp us with a putative
identity. Lost is our ability to *vow* to be this or that, vows coordinated
through our people's rites and customs with the wheeling seasons of the
universe. Thus made, vows are embedded in our core.

Joseph, defeated chief of the Nez Perce people—

> From where the sun now stands, I will fight no more forever.[4]

James detected that sore, that wound, that all our science and quasi-
science, technology and methodology, scientific linguistics and semantics
can conceal but cannot heal: the inability to be firm, centered, confident in
our inherently expansive, ecstatic, and responsible being day by day.

Let us focus on that academic field that some might expect to pursue
the question of being: philosophy. Aristotle declared that it is this question
that has always been, and will always be, asked. But enlightened "scientific" thinkers, authorized now by national professional associations, seem
to know better. Only a few philosophers have raised the question of being
in this century, for example, James in *Some Problems of Philosophy*, Heidegger in many places, and, implicitly, Dewey and the later Wittgenstein.

Most of the rest just assume that the question of being is too vague or abstract. It must be replaced with specific questions that can be handled by specific methodologies. Lacking a centered sense of themselves as vital members of the whole, they fail to see that Aristotle's question of being applied to our times might (with some imagination) allow a coordinated view, which, gathering things together, would encourage *coherence and concreteness.*

Whereas in Aristotle's vision quantity and quality are essential aspects of the ground of being, in the scientist-philosophers from the seventeenth century on they fly apart. When universities were professionalized in the last decades of the nineteenth century, they were partitioned and constituted along the lines of dualisms or polar oppositions integral to seventeenth century scientific and "scientific" thought.[5] These are eccentric bifurcations in which one side or the other is given precedence as a result of whatever wind of doctrine or individual whim is blowing at the moment: subjective/objective—which matches qualitative/quantitative—and self/ other, individual/group, mind/matter, rational/irrational, present/past, male/female, and so on. Professors live embedded in these mental, and now institutional, structures. No fiddling with managerial arrangements in the university can move them out of this semitrance.

I have just concluded a course called Philosophy in Literature. Students majoring both in philosophy and in English complained of their experience in the university over several years: each field was obsessed with the technical apparatus and glossary of terms distinctive to it. Subject matter of the greatest human concern was peripheralized or eclipsed by the shiny tools that ought to have revealed it. The students' university experience fell to pieces.

This must happen when an organic sense of the whole falls away, leaving the quantitative and the qualitative disconnected, and when inquirers lose a sense of their own centers as existing beings. Individuation cannot be a vital matter of responsibly placing and conducting ourselves as whole living things in the whole world, but must be decided by externals: the current methodologies of professional-academic disciplines that define and individuate themselves nationally and internationally in the information business (and by which young professionals must be certified if they would advance in the business). For a prime example, anthropologists arrive uninvited in the front yards of indigenous peoples and expect them to submit themselves as objects for scientific investigation. The researchers assume superior knowledge and a kind of divine right—indeed, obligation—to understand these others.[6]

Across academia it is assumed that all issues are questions formulable in some specialized vocabulary or other, and that the only responsible way to get the big picture is to add up the results from each field. But the summing somehow never takes place. The possibility of other questions, perhaps better questions, is concealed, and the concealment concealed.

When this kind of presumption reigns in the field of philosophy, the results are particularly fatuous and absurd. A kind of scientism pervades the most seemingly various philosophical coteries. To reiterate: this is the view, unsupportable by science, that only science can know (or some conceptual activities somehow associated with science or appearing sharp and precise and "scientific").[7] When it presumes hegemony, it just assumes that art, religion, "literary" history, commonsense and everyday intuition cannot know essential aspects of reality. This is fanaticism and dogmatism every bit as rank and brash as ever religious organization exhibited, and, indeed, without religion's cover story about the ultimate mystery of things.

Professional philosophers today commonly assume that logical positivism, with its uncritical reliance upon the science of the day, is dead. This is self-congratulatory delusion, the fruit of a scientistic faith in progress. For example, the positivistic opposition between the emotive and the cognitive informs at a subterranean level much of the cross-over work of philosophers and cognitive scientists. Take Steven Pinker's *How the Mind Works*.[8] He advances interesting ideas about understanding human mind in terms of "reverse engineering": we see that adaptations to environments have been achieved, and define our task as explaining the means by which these have come about. And certain computer models of information processing are provided that have some value.

But Pinker finds music making—universal, fundamental in all cultures—to be anomalous. Which means there must be something basically wrong or missing in his view. James could have told him what it is: To miss the joy is to miss all. Pinker's work exhibits "the haunting unreality of 'realistic' books."[9] The fusion of reality and ideal novelty excites and empowers us, and does so because we are organisms which, to be vital, must celebrate our being. On this level we are not all that different from chimpanzees who, I have heard, feel a storm coming on, resonate to it, and do their marvelous rain dance in which, perhaps, they celebrate the bare fact of just being in a universe of such power.

The rhythms, melodies, harmonies, phrasings of our music are part and parcel of this celebration of bodily and personal being within a processual, rhythmic, participatory universe. Intensifying, clarifying, confirming our feeling-experiencing in typical situations, music develops our capacities for adaptation. Not to see it as biologically significant is to artificially separate the so-called hard or objective sciences from the so-called subjective domain of the mind. Only thinkers lost in scientism and the information business could fail to see it, or glimpsing it, find it anomalous. They've read too much in *Mind* perhaps and not lived enough in mindful and grateful celebration. Dostoevsky defined the modern human as the ungrateful animal, and Heidegger tried to cultivate *denken als danken*, thinking as thanking.

But they no more than James are mainstream philosophers today. What passes as education is not the *educing* (*educare*) of our needs, yearnings, questionings as beings who must develop ourselves or rot in boredom—or spin out of orbit in eccentricity. But it is rather *instruction* in data and the methods for amassing more of it: *instruere*, structuring-into. Such has a place, of course; but without a vital sense of the organic whole we don't know what that place is.

Or take the old positivist cut dividing "doing philosophy" from "doing the history of philosophy." The latter has a place within "scientific" philosophy, for it is construed as the scientific study of the past: scholarly antiquarianism with its apparatus of relevant languages and literature searches, etc. This cut is still commonly made, and historians in the field of philosophy stand firm for the paltry degree of respectability still possible for them.

For William James this division is artificial and stultifying. As we saw, all meaning and truth are a species of goodness, and this is the fruitful building out of the past into the present and future. Meaning-making and truth are essential features of being vitally alive and centered, of fully being, and philosophy is meant to nurture and feed us—we who are ecstatic body-minds.

Professionalized philosophy has done exactly what James said in 1903 it would do: it distends and dissociates us from our moral and psychical centers as persons. Endless ill-formed and fruitless debates, for instance, over "determinism or freedom," have sapped human energies and burdened library shelves. James responds to the existential crisis that is upon us. We should grasp tightly the question of freedom as we actually confront it in life. Many of our undergraduates want us and need us to do this, afflicted as they frequently are with addictions and despair.

But the question of freedom cannot be grasped within some concocted framework of abstractions that passes as scientific detachment and objectivity. That way, we have already gone out of touch with our immediate experience of ourselves. We must pose the question in a way that doesn't beg it against freedom.

In his *Talks to Teachers* ("The Will")[10] James argues in the fitting way: logically and scientifically speaking—really scientifically speaking—to *wait* for evidence for *freedom* is nonsensical. *If* we are free, the first act of freedom should be to freely believe in free will!

This is the heart of what Ralph Barton Perry happily meant in his title, *In the Spirit of William James*. It is thinking charged with the spirit of adventure that refuses to be trapped in dualisms or in hypostatized abstractions or noun phrases like "the mind." That refuses to get caught in a verbalism like "the mind turning in upon itself." That escapes the self-deception of an act of reflection and analysis unaware of itself that mistakes its artifacts for building blocks of knowledge and life. I mean, of course, putative sense data, images, sensations that act like a screen that divides us from the world that formed us over millions of years, and that still sustains us every moment—though that is greatly easy to forget.

James's notion of pure or neutral experience is no mere academic-intellectual exercise. Understanding it is vital for grasping learning, knowing, and being—education. In reconnecting and reinvolving us consciously with the matrix of the earth within which we took shape over many millennia, James reintroduces us to the oldest forms of religious and healing orientation within the world. (See particularly the early chapters in my *The Primal Roots of American Philosophy*, in which I connect James's idea of pure experience and the healing methods of the Native American shaman, Black Elk. Also see Essay 4 in this volume.)

Education today must be ecological. This is not because it is fashionable to be this, but because it is physically and spiritually necessary for our lives. In 1998 a marvelous book appeared: *The Spirit of Regeneration: Andean Culture Confronting Western Notions of Development*.[11] It offers articles by Peruvian intellectuals who are returning to their Andean roots after discovering the limitations, or worse, of Western notions of development. These are sweeping formulae of agribusiness and international trade that ride roughshod over the local knowledge of growing, nurturing, and living that has funded itself over 10,000 years in the Andes. There is a web of life, of concrete coherence, in which everything converses with and nourishes everything else: greatly various gods, goddesses, animals, climatic regions and altitudes, seasons, stars, the sun and moon. Or the color, taste, texture of soils, and the two thousand-plus species of potato that the people nourish and that nourish the people and that outnumber the pestilences or climatic anomalies that might strike any particular species. Talk of Clifford Geertz's "local knowledge"! These Peruvian intellectuals are deprofessionalizing themselves.

I am inspired by this. Along with Ivan Illich, for example, I think we must both deprofessionalize and deschool ourselves if we would break out of a mindless secular catechism.

Before making any proposals for restructuring the university, we should be sure that the heart of James's vision is securely in place. Otherwise the status quo perpetuates itself furtively, that is, the managing mania, what Mary Daly calls methodolatry. James's is the vision of human life as freedom, of human life as ecstatic.

In that impossible book which somehow did get written, *The Varieties of Religious Experience,* James wonders what we contact in religious or mystical experience. He thinks that on its "hither side" it is our own subconscious minds (whatever that means exactly). On its "farther side"? He echoes Emerson's notion of the horizon and the beyond it entails. James can only say it is "the more." That is all that can honestly be described. We touch the domain of what we don't know we don't know.

To attempt to follow the flow of our feeling into this "more," into its richness, depths, and shadowy surroundings, is to be free. It cannot be followed in our everyday mode of awareness for it does not present itself as an action-oriented movement. It is a kind of abandonment, a way of being that is allowing, a choice that would encompass and facilitate all further choices.

James's student, William Ernest Hocking, asserted that the original sin is the failure of awareness. The language is not too strong. For the difficulty, the failure of awareness, cannot be attacked by individuals, no matter how sharp and sincere and responsible they might be. A lack of awareness cannot be remedied on command: when *awareness* is lacking we cannot be aware of just what is missing, just what must be achieved by just what means. We face the essential finitude of human being—how we conceal the fact of concealment itself, and how we typically overlook the very possibility of our self-deceptions and our limitations.

Like Socrates, James stings us into wakefulness with respect to our tedious hungers and our tunnel-vision mind games. He italicizes situations in which we cannot escape choice, in which opportunities will never come again, and in which not to choose is to choose. The ultimate forced option is, Will we choose to wake up?

But, again, it is not a choice to achieve an end by such and such means. It must be a kind of strange choice, a metachoice, to be trusting and vulnerable, to be open to the unexpectable, to inarticulable possibilities of nonbeing and to unimaginable possibilities of being. Finally, open to the possibility that ends all the others, death. Only open this far can we be willing to give up stupid habits and to be open transformatively to new possibilities.

James suggests that we exist most of the time in profound, stupefying self-deception, and without awareness of this cramped, viscous state, all talk of education is sillibub, flattery, and spongecake. The world is meaningful, his philosophy of pure experience teaches us, because it is experienceable in various ways. But as meaningful, as experienced and experienceable by me, the world has always had me in it! How can *I* die, *not* be?

The good teacher and learner is always prodding us out of this deadening self-deception, this dribbling out of our lives. The prodding cannot be direct, for then we, the prodded, raise our defenses and fearfully block the dilation of consciousness into "the more." This holds the dim and dreaded real possibility (focal at some moments) that we are incredibly fragile and ephemeral, existing for a few moments within the vast ongoing universe that spawned us, generation after generation, over millions of years—existing for a few moments and then gone.

James sidles up beside us and nudges us toward awareness. His "On a Certain Blindness in Human Beings" is mainly stories—by R. L. Stephenson, W. H. Hudson, Walt Whitman, and others. As if only stories, not our desiccating Cartesian epistemologies, could put us in touch with what most needs to be known, ourselves. But in his own gnomic—better, shamanic—voice he sometimes meets us:

> When your ordinary Brooklynite or New Yorker, leading a life replete with too much luxury, or tired and careworn about his personal affairs, crosses the ferry or goes up Broadway, his fancy does not "soar away into the sunset" as did Whitman's, nor does he inwardly realize at all the indisputable fact

that this world never did anywhere or at any time contain more of essential divinity, or of eternal meaning, than is embodied in the field of vision over which his eyes so carelessly pass. There is life; and there, a step away, is death.[12]

To acknowledge death, to acknowledge it in one's body, is to be freed to the preciousness of each moment of life. If we are aware, just to be is joyous. "For to miss the joy is to miss all. In the joy of the actors lies the sense of any action." James is drawing from Stephenson: "His life from without may seem but a rude mound of mud: there will be some golden chamber at the heart of it, in which he dwells delighted."

Any proposals to reorganize the university not predicated on the principle that to miss the joy is to miss all perpetuate the iron cage of bureaucracy, business as usual. That is, finding tenure track jobs in "the best departments" for bright young Ph.D. students; our endless unreeling of technical expertise to lure approval from authorities in the professional association; all the ephemeral pleasures of the engineering mentality that has lost touch with poetical and musical sensibility, with real, troubling, human concerns, and with ecstatic transports and joys. To miss the joy of just being is to sit starved in some cage or other, gilded though it may be.

Professional attitudes are incarnated in, and controlled by, national academic associations, for example, The American Philosophical Association. It is a rigid pecking order that controls many of the prestigious jobs (in an ever shrinking pool) and nearly all grant money, because referees for all occasions are picked from the top of the hierarchy. Those outside it are invisible. It is not too much to say that they are untouchable. Each academic field, from English to physics, has its own professional association and is pretty well defined by it.

The academic world is segmented into bureaus. This stifles creativity, even minimal general education. A graduate student properly professionalized in philosophy, say, will tend nearly always to miss the philosophical content in both the literary and scientific domains (although given the ruling "analytic" philosophy, which fancies itself to be scientific, there is slightly less chance of missing philosophical content and issues in the sciences).

It is hard for generally informed citizens to believe, but it is true: Figures whom they themselves probably recognize to be philosophers may not be recognized to be such by the best and the brightest Ph.D. products of the best and the brightest philosophy departments. I mean household names like R. W. Emerson and Henry Thoreau, not to mention "merely literary" figures such as Dostoevsky or Tolstoy or Melville, or "religious figures" like Kierkegaard, or "sociologists" such as Max Weber. Preening, shameless, unabashed parochialism parading as clarity, science, and enlightenment presents a nearly incredible spectacle. Everyone suffers, most obviously students who hunger for ecstatic connectedness, the creation of meaning and their own being. Dominant analytic philosophers betray the trust the public places in them (insofar as the public is aware of them at all).

To miss the joy is to miss all. By joy I mean specifically the moral-ecstatic energy of the creation of meaning across received boundaries. To leave out of account this missing joy as one tries to reconstruct the university is to be caught up in flailings and fumblings and exhaustions that miss the central point, the heart of education itself: the creative eliciting and forming of self. It is idolatry shrouded in good intentions—methodolatry.

We should not proceed further without mentioning a cautionary historical fact. When the American Philosophical Association was being organized in 1901, an invitation to join (and probably to be elected president) was issued to William James. He replied that he expected little to come from professionalizing what should, he said, be the patient conversation between trusted friends and colleagues. "Count me out," he replied curtly. Very soon, however, two younger philosophers—John Dewey and Josiah Royce—were elected president. James promptly changed his mind about joining and was elected.[13]

Well, well, what does this prove? What we should know and remember all along: Human, all too human. There is no underestimating human vanity. Nor the fear of being unrecognized and erased and deprived of power to resist a world in which we dimly but truly apprehend ourselves to exist precariously every moment. Not even a famous Harvard professor from a famous family is immune. (James was particularly prone to jealousy with regard to accomplished younger men, as his ambivalent attitude toward his brother, the novelist and dramatist Henry Jr., amply attests. Consult Leon Edel's massive biography of Henry.)[14]

I will sketch some steps we might take to reorganize the university to bring it closer to what the public thinks it is already, an educational institution. Each step presupposes a new attitude toward the University. The birthright of all humans should be the opportunity to develop each one's capacities to the utmost, to experience the joy of having these capacities touched, educed, drawn out (*educare*). Just by virtue of being human, everyone has a stake in the university, an idea beautifully elaborated in Henry Rosovsky's *The University: An Owner's Manual.*[15] From the most frightened freshman to the most exalted dean, everyone's voice must contribute to the drama of what we are to make of ourselves.

Once the first seeds of a new attitude and its new expectations sprout, perhaps the first structural move should be to eliminate the philosophy department. All fields, pursued to their conceptual foundations, involve philosophical assumptions and commitments, however implicit. This was the original rationale for the Doctor of Philosophy degree: anyone who does any creative work in the foundations of any received discipline should receive the ultimate recognition of intellectual distinction. And in fact some of the most important intellectual work in the last centuries has been done by people who would not be employed in philosophy departments. Just a few: Darwin, Freud, Jung, Einstein, Bohr, Pauli, Heisenberg, Mann, Borges. And, especially more recently, an emerging group of women would also not; to mention a few: Elizabeth Cady Stanton, Jane Ellen Harrison, Willa Cather, Marija Gimbutas, Julia Kristeva, Luci Irigary, Toni Morrison, Leslie Marmon Silko.

To eliminate philosophy departments would not entail dismissing the members of the department. They should be left free to associate themselves with whatever departments are closest to their interests and accomplishments. And they would, presumably, associate themselves with members whose interests are closest to theirs. In some cases, adroit administrators would be needed to find a proper home for some professors of philosophy.

I would also suggest that each member of the university, tenured and untenured, be required to deliver a presentation every five years to the intellectual community of the university at large. Inevitably, in speaking across departmental lines, thinkers would dwell on assumptions and issues relevant to all fields, that is, on philosophical matters.

In the end, we should proceed to a completely decompartmentalized and deprofessionalized university as rapidly as we wisely can. That is, to a *university* that lives up to the literal meaning of the name: that which has a center and turns around it—the creation of meaning, the discovery and husbanding of truth, and the development of centered and expansive persons. What would remain would be a very few general fields, defined in greatly overlapping terms, and headed by universal minds who appear now and again in the strangest places. Consider Isaiah Berlin, Albert Einstein, James Conant, Susanne Langer, or William James himself.

The present situation has reduced itself to absurdity. Yes, there is overlap today between philosophy departments and cognitive science departments, say. But this itself is eccentric, and produces grossly incomplete views of "mind," such as Steven Pinker's. Beyond this is the patently absurd. Please look again at the Leiter Report, the ranking of analytic philosophy departments. In itself it might be considered trivial, the work of a fairly recent Ph.D. from Michigan State, a one man gang, so to say. But nothing exists merely in itself. As I said in the previous essay, The Report has had considerable impact, given the vanity and fear of human beings, and their need to belong in powerful groups.[16] Nothing better indicates the lack of confidence in one's own judgment, particularly analytic philosophers' lack of centeredness in their own situated, bodily, and willing-feelingful existence, and, concomitantly, their inability to ground their evaluations in intellectual history—even their own intellectual history.[17]

It is not only their failure, but also that of university personnel in positions of power. How can deans, for example, allocating funds and professorial positions to their colleges, and themselves trained very often in the "best" multiversities today, be expected to know what is happening in the various professional-academic worlds? Evaluations and assignments, however, must be made, and they will be—within whatever flimsy frameworks for ranking are available, and however incredibly short is the time given them to evaluate the university's needs.

The slightest knowledge of intellectual history, and the barest confidence in one's own judgment, shows that the most creative advances in knowledge and appreciation occur not in mainstream departments, but in the foggy overlap areas between disciplines. Or in areas that have not yet been mapped out and given a name, but in which individuals exercise their intuition, invention, perseverance. (I think, for example, of the recent discovery by Francine Shapiro of eye-movement therapy for emotional trauma.)[18]

It is time that the iron cage of academic bureaucracy be dismantled. The progress of knowledge itself requires it. Even more obviously, students' hunger for meaning, and the whole society's call for integration and council, are too urgent to allow dawdling. As Emerson prophesied would be increasingly the case (with even the words picked up by Nietzsche),

The state of society is one in which the members have suffered amputation from the trunk, and strut about so many walking monsters,—a good finger, a neck, stomach, an elbow, but never a man.[19]

William James is closer to us than are either Emerson or Nietzsche. It is his warnings—as a man of science, of common sense, and of wide and humane learning—that we should most directly heed.

I have written centrally about the degeneration of academic philosophy in the university. But this is a bellwether discipline: mandarinism and vitiation here reflect hyperspecialization, frivolousness, and flaccidness across the culture. A necessary condition for recovery is to place as much emphasis on rebuilding education and educators as was placed on rebuilding Japan and Germany after World War II. Or an emphasis now on spending billions to bail out nations that have collapsed economically. We should send a vast Peace Corps into the public schools, reward persons with compassionate hearts and good minds and the toughness of Green Berets, and give master teachers their economic and social due. We should pay the tired, weary, and demoralized—tired, weary, demoralized for good reason—to retire early. The present situation is an insult to us all.

I agree with James Garrison, a professor of education, who has written in a personal communication:

What I found in education was a world of wonderfully dedicated kindergarten through twelfth grade teachers controlled by bureaucracy, downtrodden by dead but dominant versions of technocratically applied positivism, . . . and scape-goated for their efforts in ameliorating social ills.

We should unpack the notion of social ills. Both William James and John Dewey knew that science and technology must inevitably develop, but that there was much more required for a fulfilled life than they could supply. Despite all our interventions, inventions, conventions, we still belong to Nature. Despite all our clever turnings of attention and employment of technological fixes, the vast matrix of our lives is involuntary (as Schopenhauer, Nietzsche, James, Freud, and Dewey knew). As things are going, the malcoordination of the voluntary and the involuntary only increases. A corollary: the malcoordination of the cultural and the natural only increases.

In their somewhat different styles, James and Dewey see that for thought to be effective it must be both pragmatic and primal. The tragic feature of Dewey's thought is that he knew that modern life had introduced dissociations on the subconscious level of minding, but his deployment of critical thought penetrates to this level only sporadically. Art can do some important knitting together here, Dewey saw. Body-work, of the Alexander variety, say, can do some more. But Dewey could not supply a wholly viable alternative to ages-old myth and ritual, could not suture together science, technology, and "individual fate lore," could not reintegrate Father Sky and Mother Earth, as Black Elk might have put it.[20] Dewey quotes Matthew Arnold on contemporary persons as

> wandering between two worlds, one dead,
> The other powerless to be born.

Perhaps the old world is not as dead as Dewey and Arnold thought, and perhaps a Socratic project of midwifery to the new world should be seriously considered.

James's tragedy is several faceted. He saw that belief—indeed, belief beyond presently available evidence, over-belief—is essential for a sound and coherent life. But he himself had great difficulty believing. It took a tremendous effort of will to sustain him in what he called the strenuous life, particularly as life ebbed out of him in sickness and advancing age. Some of us understand this only too well.

A reader complained that the present essay goes way beyond what is supported by James. Since some (perhaps not well acquainted with James) might agree, I add a few final words.

I imagine that if James could see what has happened to education at the end of this century he would denounce it more eloquently and damningly than I ever could. Here is exactly how he responded in 1901 to the invitation to join the fledgling American Philosophical Association:

> I don't foresee much good from a philosophical society. Philosophy discussion proper only succeeds between intimates who have learned how to converse by months of weary trial and failure. The philosopher is a beast dwelling in his individual burrow. Count me *out!*[21]

True, as I've noted, James joined the APA and was elected president in 1905. But his better self is evident in his initial refusal. He knew from long experience with the likes of Charles Peirce and Josiah Royce that philosophers best converse with intimates through months of weary trial and failure. This is so because we grope for meaning, and we must trust others to listen patiently, and to show us if they can where we go wrong, and to help us to go right. How would James react to the greatly impersonal and rushed atmosphere of academic philosophy today? I think he would be appalled.

There is a profound difficulty for professionalized thought of all kinds. Professionalization sets up a vast machinery of evaluation of submitted work. It seems self-evident today that work should be blind reviewed, and by more than one person.

But not everyone judged to be a competent reviewer will detect very creative work the first time through it. Maybe one or two readers will reject it. And this will very probably kill it. For most editors of the "best" publications, it seems obvious that one black ball in the urn is like a fly in the ointment, an infection, a desecration. "We publish only the best!"

Despite a surface show of innovation and adventure, built into most of our academic institutions today is a stupefying conservatism. It was evident to Emerson before James was born. On "The American Scholar:"

> [The scholar] must relinquish display and immediate fame [and in creating and discovering endure] the self-accusation . . . the frequent uncertainty and loss of time . . . the state of virtual hostility in which he seems to stand to society, especially to educated society.[22]

To use a distinction made famous by Thomas Kuhn, academia on all levels tends to reward competent but conventional thought, and tends to discourage revolutionary thought—what we desperately need to survive, as individuals and as a species.

All this is hard to stomach for academics who, for the most part, have been rewarded for their competent but conventional work. But if we want change we will have to bite the bullet, maybe even swallow it whole. Note the notorious case of discrimination against regenerative and revolutionary thought: the persecution and exclusion of Charles Peirce, probably the most brilliant mind (along with Jefferson) that the United States has produced. Good biographies have finally appeared, so that only a few of the most salient facts need be recounted: the vengeful pursuit of Peirce over 40 years by the president of Harvard, Charles Eliot; Peirce's betrayal by the now nearly forgotten astronomer, Simon Newcomb (who, among other things, scuttled Peirce's application for a desperately needed Smithsonian fellowship); his dismissal as Assistant Professor at Johns Hopkins on vague grounds of impropriety.

I'll begin to close with lines from the obituary of Peirce written by Joseph Jastrow, ninth president of the American Psychological Association! I wish it could serve as an obituary for education as we know it.

> It cannot but remain a sad reflection upon the organization of our academic interest that we find it difficult, or make it so, to provide places for exceptional men within the academic fold. Politically as educationally, we prefer the safe men to the brilliant men, and exact a versatile mediocrity of qualities that make the individual organizable. . . . Certainly it remains true for all times that no more effective stimulus to promising young minds can be found than to give them the opportunity of contact with master minds in action. The service that a small group of such men can perform is too fine, too imponderable, to be measured; and likewise too intangible to impress its value upon the judgment of those with whom these issues commonly lie.[23]

Most educational institutions today focus on organizing the individual. Standardized tests typify this: they lend an aura of objectivity and reliability to cloak a profound anxiety about what's truly important for knowers to know and to be. The discipline that should epitomize unfettered and unabashed mind, philosophy, has become self-absorbed (just what James and Max Weber said would happen): inhibited, crabbed, professionalized practically beyond belief. Analytic philosophers in "the best" institutions shut themselves off from the history of philosophy (even in the West) and also from profoundly philosophical ecological and educational debates raging around us. They shut themselves up in self-congratulatory coteries and convince themselves that they can decisively rank individuals and departments. The musty smell is plain to everyone except the occupants of the closets. Never before has William James's thought and example been more needed. His work throws open windows and doors. He prompts us to see where we are truly alive: in the unknown.

Notes

1. "The Ph.D. Octopus," *Essays, Comments, and Reviews, The Works of William James* (Cambridge, MA: Harvard University Press, 1987), p. 69. The essay

can be found in *Memories and Studies* (New York: Longmens, Green & Co., 1911 [1903]), and is included in the main in my anthology, *William James: The Essential Writings* (Albany: SUNY Press, 1984 [1971]).

2. These quotations from Kierkegaard, Nietzsche, Dostoevsky are, respectively, *Journals* (February 7, 1846); "Schopenhauer as Educator" (in *Untimely Meditations*); *Crime and Punishment* (from the mouth of Svidrigailov, pt. 5, sec. 5), and, of course, *The Underground Man* (the first pages). I trust the reader will pardon me for not giving more detailed annotation. These are famous books, each in numerous editions. But in an essay of this bent, to give detailed annotation? The writers would have loved the irony: an essay encumbered with heavy scholarly apparatus critical of scholarly inertia and apparatus!

3. See, for example, "Bureaucracy," *From Max Weber: Essays in Sociology* edited by H. H. Gerth & C. Wright Mills (New York: Oxford University Press, 1946), sec. VIII.

4. This justly famous vow can be found in many sources, e.g., *War Chief Joseph*, by H. A. Howard and D. L. McGrath (Lincoln: University of Nebraska Press, 1964 [1941]), p. 282.

5. See my *The Moral Collapse of the University: Professionalism, Purity, Alienation* (Albany: State University of New York Press, 1990), especially pp. 37 ff.

6. Recently, certain anthropologists have exhibited greater sensitivity to their research "subjects." But even if culturally disruptive trade goods—gifts to elicit information from informants—are discontinued, the very act of studying and objectifying cultures is alienating for them (and also for the Westerners doing the studying). However, given the ever encroaching commercial interests of North Atlantic culture ("globalization") there is little even the best-intentioned anthropologists can do to protect indigenous peoples.

7. See my *Wild Hunger: The Primal Roots of Modern Addiction*, cited in the first essay, indexed under "scientism."

8. Steven Pinker, *How the Mind Works* (New York: W. W. Norton, 1997), pp. 534–537.

9. See James, "On a Certain Blindness in Human Beings," in *The Will to Believe* (New York: Dover Books, 1956 [1897]). Also in my anthology, *William James: The Essential Writings*. I believe music is a primal adaptation. When normal body-selves respond adaptively to the "outer" environment, or take initiatives with respect to it, the body resounds fittingly within itself. Music is feed-out/feed-back that conducts, confirms, orients body-self, underwrites its identity through time. It has done this from time immemorial. Pinker's dualistic talk about the mind renders him incapable of grasping how music is primally adaptive, a motor of evolution: he generates a pseudoproblem of identity. As thinkers, we are left not

fully engaged with our bodies, not fully engaged with our capacities for ecstatic life. This furthers contemporary alienation and disintegration of identity. How ironical for a self-styled evolutionary approach to self! Despite some interesting science, the overall effect of Pinker's work is scientism.

10. *Talks to Teachers on Psychology and to Students on Some of Life's Ideals* (New York: H. Holt, 1915 [1899]), p. 252. Also to be found in my anthology, just cited.

11. *The Spirit of Regeneration* (London and New York: Zed Books, 1998; distributed by St. Martin's Press). Edited and introduced by Frederique Apffel-Marglin.

12. William James, *Talks to Teachers*. Also to be found in my anthology, just cited.

13. Quoted in Edward I. Pitts, "Ideals & Reality: The Early Years of the American Philosphical Association," p. 2. This is excerpted from his dissertation, Penn State University, 1979,and was delivered as a paper to the Society for the Advancement of American Philosophy, 1980.

14. Leon Edel, *Henry James: The Conquest of London, The Middle Years, The Treacherous Years,* in 3 vols. (New York: Avon Books, 1976). A strand through these volumes traces the brothers' relationship.

15. Henry Rosovsky, *The University: An Owner's Manual* (New York: W. W. Norton, 1991).

16. A frothy article by Christopher Shea details the controversy that has finally arisen over the report, in *Linguafranca: The Review of Academic Life* (July/August 1999).

17. Nonanalytic approaches are lumped under the heading, "Continental." This apparently exhaustive set of alternatives completely occludes the whole tradition of American philosophy—a third alternative.

18. Francine Shapiro (with Margot Silk Forrest), *EMDR: Eye Movement Desensitization and Reprocessing* (New York: Basic Books, 1997).

19. "The American Scholar," in L. Ziff, ed., *R. W. Emerson: Selected Essays* (New York: Penguin Books, p. 84).

20. See Dewey's *The Problems of Men* (New York: Philosophical Library, 1946), especially the articles on William James (where Dewey uses the phrase "individual fate lore"), and the Introduction. The Introduction to *Problems of Men* is found in the critical edition, edited by Jo Ann Boydston *John Dewey, The Later Works, 1925–1953,* vol. 15 (Carbondale: Southern Illinois University Press, 1989), p. 154. Dewey contrasts "the secular" to "the theological" and "the supernatural." But there is a meaning of "religion" that falls into neither camp, and it is just this meaning that is relevant for understanding the native American, Black Elk, as well

as Thoreau, Emerson, and James. "The Philosophy of William James," written originally as a review in 1937 can (with effort) be found in the critical edition, *John Dewey, The Later Works, 1925–1953,* vol. 11, 1935–37, pp. 464–478. I thank John McDermott for help in finding my way in the critical editions of James and Dewey. (The critical edition of James does not include a general index to the series; the Dewey does, but in listing works chronologically it breaks up materials included together in previous editions. An aid to learning?)

21. See note #13 and also my *The Moral Collapse of the University* (Albany: SUNY Press, 1990), pp. 106–107.

22. Again, in Ziff, *Selected Essays,* pp. 95–96, and quoted in my *The Moral Collapse,* p. 88.

23. Quoted in K. L. Ketner, *His Glassy Essence: An Autobiography of Charles Sanders Peirce* (Nashville: Vanderbilt University Press, 1998), p. 29.

N.B.: A version of this essay was published in my *The Primal Roots of American Philosophy: Pragmatism, Phenomenology, and Native American Thought* (University Park: Penn State University Press, 2000). Another version will appear in *William James's Philosophy of Education,* ed. by J. Garrison, *et. al.,* (New York: Teachers College Press, 2002).

3

The Pluralist Rebellion in the
American Philosophical Association

Since the 1930s, academic philosophy in the United States has become increasingly professionalized, increasingly dominated by its academic professional organization, The American Philosophical Association. As I pointed out in my book, *The Moral Collapse of the University: Professionalism, Purity, Alienation* (1990), academics are not insulated from the general movement of culture toward hyperspecialization and the dogmatic adherence to scientific and technological progress. In the case of philosophy, this amounts to scientism: the belief that only science can know. As I've repeatedly pointed out, science cannot know that only it can know; it is not a scientific position.

In the last 70 years, much past philosophical thought has been ridiculed—implicitly or explicitly—by the academic philosophical establishment. When I was writing my dissertation nearly 40 years ago, William James tended to be dismissed as a lightweight. (My major professors, William Barrett and Sidney Hook, were two of the few exceptions to the general climate—though Hook spoke critically of James's tenderness toward people's "over-beliefs," beliefs exceeding currently available evidence.)

This has begun to change a little. But not much in the great centers of academic-philosophical professionalism: the analytic departments in "the best" graduate schools. I wrote the following in 1985 or 86. It describes how some of us took on the establishment and perhaps changed the course of history a teeny bit. It was never published before; nobody was much interested in publishing it. Perhaps it was not politically correct. I include it for its historical as well as current significance.

Those of us who have participated in the APA in the last several decades—and done so with the detachment (or is it alienation?) necessary for perspective—know the power of the group to mimetically condition its members to think that the nutshell in which they live is the whole world. It is the mimetic as the hermetic. From the 1930s through the 1970s, the fateful dynamic unfolded itself: a method for producing marketable results totalizes itself, achieves monopoly status—and purity—and shoves to the sidelines and stigmatizes competing purveyors. They are excreted and ignored. Some on the sidelines keep looking in, however.

When the dynamic of professionalism carries away philosophers, the spectacle achieves a peculiar vividness, pathos, and absurdity. Call it tragic farce. For philosophers are paid and tenured to think for themselves. They have the opportunity (one would think) to perpetually gain new perspective on the world, to pump "free air around things," as James put it. But, in fact, they did not pump free air around themselves, nor around their world, so as to achieve perspective on their own behavior.

Aristotle maintained that the common run of men live like cattle. Jesus was closer to the truth: they live like sheep. We are all quite used to this. But when the individuals present themselves as philosophers—as uncommon persons—the scene gains a tragical-farcical dimension that bugs the eyes of the beholder on the sidelines. One does not know whether to laugh, to cry, to collapse with apoplexy, or to sit down, collect oneself, and to try to describe and explain what one sees. I opt now for the latter course.

In January 1978, a number of us professors of philosophy met on a Saturday in Charles Sherover's apartment in Manhattan. We had just experienced another dreary, unpardonably parochial convention of the APA, Eastern Division. We had been sidelined for decades. Resignation and despair were deeply ingrained. There were more philosophers on the sidelines than in the game.

As a compensatory move, some of us had formed games of our own. Many fringe groups had developed: societies of metaphysics, of process studies, of phenomenology, of classical American philosophy, of sex and love, of this and that. Many of these subgroups met at ghetto hours during the APA convention. Before the official program began, or at dinner hours, abstruse scuffles would break out here and there, or more demure exchanges on esoteric topics such as the nature of reality, of being, of the self. In fact, so many peripheral societies and associations developed that the APA was in danger of implosion, collapse at its core. But so inured to ostracism had we become that we hardly imagined what might be done to change things. As Byron wrote in "The Prisoner of Chillon":

Even my chains and I grew friends,
So much long communion tends,
To make us what we are.

Stages of gradual, more or less controlled implosion of the professional organization had proceeded by increments so small and regular that even we on the sidelines had been carried along in a stupefying myopia and trance. Persons outside this field may find it difficult or impossible to believe, but by the late 1970s, nine out of ten newly minted Ph.D.'s in philosophy could not speak intelligently for two minutes on the work of the nineteenth- and twentieth-century philosophers that the rest of the lettered world deem important, for example, James, Emerson, Dewey, Thoreau, Whitehead. Many had never read cover to cover a major treatise in the history of philosophy. They had been dubbed Doctor Philosophicus mainly on the basis of reading and responding to articles in the "best" journals as these had accumulated in the last four or so decades—a store of highly perishable material. The technical proficiency with which these articles analyzed writable language was awesome, so thick, elaborate, and self-sealing that the proficiency had become the problem: it concealed fundamental philosophical options and human needs.

Who are the best philosophers? Those who read papers in the official APA program and publish in the best journals. Why is the APA official program the best forum and why are these journals the best publications? Because the best philosophers perform in them. An airtight argument, one has to admit.

The self-closing circularity and implosion was reaching the point at which it could no longer proceed gradually. We were only dimly aware of this possibility. We were styled as beaten, middle-aged, mushy, second-rate thinkers.

However, we had just been goaded in a particularly doltish way. A group of outside evaluators from the New York State Accrediting Agency had just visited the philosophy department of the New School for Social Research. This was one of the few outposts for graduate training in Continental, nonanalytic and nonpositivistic thought. Distinguished graduates taught throughout the nation (but in only a very few graduate schools). Philosopher-evaluators threatened to remove state recognition from the program, to effectively shut it down. One of the chief grounds was that the curriculum was too specialized.

Evaluators from the nutshell world had judged that one of the very few schools that allowed graduate students another option, some breadth of choice for study, was too narrow. *It* was too narrow! They assumed that analytic and neo-positivistic methods constituted the whole range of philosophy, and then had broken this down into many subspecialties which added up, they believed, to a broad and balanced program. What found no place within this confined area was to be excreted and left to disintegrate.

We felt the goad and began meeting regularly. Older philosophers, eminent but abandoned for thirty or forty years—sealed up in the wall and left for dead—joined us. We tried to get our bearings and to figure out which way to go. We sent letters protesting the New School plight to friends outside our immediate group. The response was gratifying. Many scores of philosophers signed these letters. We were emboldened to keep meeting. We called ourselves the Saturday Group.

Late in November, it occurred to us that we should give philosophers outside New York City a chance to join us. What better opportunity than at the upcoming APA meeting just after Christmas? Although it was very late to reserve a room for a meeting, Don Ihde volunteered to try to round up something in time for an impromptu meeting. No time was left to mail an announcement.

At the last minute we found a room and the meeting was scheduled for 1 P.M. of the second day of the convention in Washington, D.C. At 9:30 the night before, I boarded a plane in Los Angeles after spending Christmas with members of family. It occurred to me that I had no idea of what to say at our meeting. Given the perennial tailwind to the East, the trip was to last only three hours and fifty minutes. My mind was sluggish. But then, through the murk, a few pages appeared on the pad. I slept from 5:30 to 10 A.M. in a Washington hotel room.

The assigned room was quite large. Standing at the front of it at 1 P.M., I felt a bit giddy and suspended. Not many would show up, I feared. We could only rely upon word of mouth. Sherover perched on his chair like the Buddha, smoked his pipe, and made remarks under his breath. This was reassuring. Quentin Lauer of Fordham huffed and puffed into the room. "I had a hard time driving through the traffic, but I'm here!" John Smith of Yale sat in his chair and radiated good humor. Before long the room was filled with well over a hundred people, my remarks were made, a sheet to establish a mailing list was circulated by Sherover. We were now "The Pluralists," and as the meeting broke up, we walked in a tattered group to the business meeting of the APA. We had no clear idea of what we would do, but we would do something. A corporate individual was being born, as inevitably as anything which is to be born gets born.

Of the approximately two thousand members of the Association attending the convention in those days, only about sixty or so usually attended the business meeting. The apathy was understandable, for seldom were issues actually raised and decided on the floor of the business meeting. Our constitution specified that officers be elected at the yearly business meeting, but in practice there was no contest. The official five-member Nominating Committee's slate was established months before and was simply confirmed in a pro forma vote. Nobody pushed for a contest—not the small, oligarchic clique of analytic philosophers who nominated each other and installed each other in the available posts year after year; not the many philosophers who used the APA's conventions to advance their own careers, who did not identify with it significantly, and did not attend the business meetings; and certainly not those who had given up and dropped out of the Association altogether.

We had heard the rumor for years that the suggestions for officers yearly solicited from the membership by the Nominating Committee had been ignored whenever they proved unpleasant: deposited in the circular file. One of our options was to move that a rule be adopted requiring that the membership be informed about who had been suggested, and by how many members. As the meeting ground to a close, "new business" appeared on the agenda, and we opted to make this motion.

The atmosphere had been primed, and now was charged. Nearly everyone sensed that something long underground had surfaced and was afoot. Kurt Baier, outgoing president, was in the chair, and his argument against the motion sounded the theme that underlay all establishment thinking: paternalism. The Nominating Committee had been duly elected (true, elected by the small number who bothered to vote each year), and that meant, he said, that those who voted entrusted the members of the committee with the power to decide matters in their wisdom. Asking them to account for their actions would be an affront.

Like a fire that draws oxygen into itself and spreads on all sides, the debate grew to include other established practices of the association. Since papers submitted to be read at the convention were reviewed blind, the author's name suppressed, it had been assumed that they were reviewed without prejudice. We rose to point out that the mere absence of the

author's name and institution did not mitigate the major source of prejudice, which was animus against methodologies and subject matters—
plainly visible in the body of the paper—not against individuals *per se.*

By the time these issues surfaced, some members had already left the
meeting. Only about fifty remained, but the atmosphere crackled. Alarm
and dismay radiated from established figures. The vote was called. As I
recall, our sunshine motion carried by a margin of twenty-six to twenty-
three.

Yet, the failure of communication and community (the numbness in
this inertial professional association) was so great that those in power did
not fully realize what they had lost. We pluralists now had the power to
make suggestions to the nominating committee and the right to ask
whether it had heeded them.

The exercise of this right is precisely what happened the following
year, Christmas 1979, at the Sheraton Hotel in New York City. We had
planned well this time, heartened by our success in Washington. We had
secured a medium-sized ballroom, circularized our growing mailing list.
The room was packed, the meeting tumultuous and festive. It was as if
time had given birth to our idea, not ourselves, and time would realize it.
Six of us spoke briefly, John Lachs of Vanderbilt closed his talk with an
irruptive, "Let's show them the door!" The hat was passed for donations, all
were informed of the momentous nature of the business meeting the next
day. We adjourned in the festive atmosphere flushed with apparent victory.

This time hundreds were now on the floor of the business meeting.
We expected that the Nominating Committee would follow its traditional
practice of making its selections from a narrow spectrum of the membership, despite our many suggestions for pluralistic candidates. Like clock-
work, the committee fulfilled our prediction. I rose on a point of order and
asked that the sunshine law be observed. Who had been suggested, and by
how many members?

Probably only a fraction of the assembly knew precisely what was
happening, but the room was so quiet that one could have heard a pin
drop. Monroe Beardsley, chair of the APA Nominating Committee, looked
stunned. The moment ballooned and still he said nothing. Finally, he
asked, "How many do you wish?" I did not understand. "How far down
the list, beginning with the person who received the greatest number of
write-ins, do you wish me to go? It's a long list."

His being stunned seemed to have communicated itself to me. Somehow, I could not come to grips with the question. Fortunately, Nicholas

Capaldi could; he turned around and showed me five fingers. "Oh, just the top five for each office will be sufficient," I said.

Beardsley, clearly, was still reluctant to read the list. In a hesitant voice he began. The top achievers for each post were not those his committee had nominated, but were precisely the ones that we were about to nominate from the floor. And, of course, this was no accident; we had written the suggestions—I assume it was mainly we. (John Smith had been nominated for executive committee by Beardsley's committee; not for president. We took this to be an attempt to divert our thrust.)

The inevitable unfolded. Our members rose from the floor, were recognized, and a counter-slate of candidates was, for the first time in APA history, nominated from the floor: John Smith for President, Quentin Lauer and John McDermott for Executive Committee, and John Lachs for Secretary. Each but the last won, and by a significant margin. Lachs lost by a whisker.

A strange, stunned pandemonium ensued. To use a vulgar locution—but a more telling one I cannot find—the shit had hit the fan. We had just elected a president of the Eastern Division of the APA, or so it appeared. Ruth Marcus, the head of the umbrella organization called the National Association of the APA and a vocal and assertive logician, looked subdued, but she was not inarticulate. She observed that there was no assurance that only members of the Eastern Division had voted. Each voter would have to have his or her membership certified. No decision could be rendered until this happened.

And, indeed, some students were on the floor. Even if they were members, they had no voting privileges. Had they voted? How about others who were members, but not members of the Eastern Division, hence likewise lacking voting privileges? Richard Rorty, the current president of the Eastern Division and chair of the meeting, ruled that a decision would have to be deferred to the next day at a special business meeting.

We were thrown into limbo. The festivity drained away. A number gave counsel and tried to cheer us up, James Edie of Northwestern and Joseph Kockelmans of Penn State among others. The anticlimax was palpable; nevertheless, we kept plugging.

It was determined that fifty-six voting cards had gone to persons not affiliated with the Eastern Division. Although no explicit commitment to *Robert's Rules of Order* is made in the bylaws of the association, we all tended to assume these were in force. In the passage most pertinent to our situation, *Robert's Rules of Order Revised* reads,

> If there is evidence that any unidentifiable ballots were cast by persons not entitled to vote, and if there is any possibility that such ballots might affect the results, the entire ballot is null and void and a new vote must be taken.

The margins of victory were less than fifty-six. But the voting cards were not ballots, as Sherover and I pointed out to Rorty in his hotel room the next morning. They were merely held aloft if the person wished to raise the hand and vote. It could not be determined who had used his or her card in which vote. But it was determined that the number of legitimate voters present exceeded the total count for the election of each officer. This was a factor to be weighed. Moreover, if the elections were to be voided, we would be left with no authorized alternative procedure for electing officers for the next year (many members would not reappear at the special business meeting, for either they could not attend or they would assume the voting was over).

Rorty was in a very difficult position. Author of the widely acclaimed *The Linguistic Turn* and numerous articles in the analytic mainstream, professor at Princeton, he had been a model professional philosopher. However, he had recently undergone an existential turn, as one might call it. He had just published his *Philosophy and the Mirror of Nature,* in which he criticized the whole scientistic movement from Descartes to the present, which assumed that all reality was, in principle, representable by clear and distinct ideas formulable in writable language and mathematics. He had gone back to James and Dewey trying to pick up threads that had been dropped and lost in the last fifty years. The rest of us might talk about this, and talk and talk, but when Rorty talked, the professional establishment had at least to cock an ear before dismissing him as having, perhaps, gone soft in the head.

As we got into a crowded elevator the next morning on the way to breakfast, a friend reached through the door and shoved a copy of the day's *New York Times* into my hands (December 30, 1979). At the head of the page, it read, "Philosophical Group's Dominant View is Criticized."[1] It was a well-written piece by Thomas Lask, reporting our meeting of the night before the election and quoting incisively from our speakers: Evelyn Shirk, "The remedy for ingrained dogmatism is pluralism"; Quentin Lauer, "Truth is too vast to be approached by any one of its facets"; and William Barrett, who, Lask wrote, "accused them of teaching in a history-less present and told of interviewing a candidate who said, as if it were a positive contribution, that he had never read a page of Whitehead"; John

Smith, who was quoted as recounting meetings years ago in which philosophers "surely disagreed, but with the differences came respect"; and others. The article closed with the statement that the Committee for Pluralism was offering its own candidates for election.[2]

Although the voting had already occurred, we still did not know the results. When the time arrived for the second business meeting, Rorty stood at the rostrum and in his peculiar monotone (the sound of infinite resignation) delivered his ruling that, because there were in all contests sufficient legitimate voters to account for the results, the election would stand. He was challenged from the floor, but this was brought to a test and defeated. Rumors of a lawsuit simmered, but nothing materialized.

To their credit, some analytic philosophers accepted the results as a chastening reminder of tasks of philosophical exploration that many of them had ignored. Others were furious. The Nominating Committee's defeated candidate, Adolph Grunbaum of Pittsburgh, had had every reason to expect to win. Our movement was shocking. It made things difficult for many people, but we saw no way to avoid this. When established figures do not regard their critics as competent, what route other than rebellion is left open?

In an effort designed evidently to prevent such irregularities at business meetings in future, it was immediately proposed by the Executive Committee of the APA Eastern that the constitution of the association be amended to allow the divisions to elect their officers in any way they chose, for example, by mail ballot. The Executive Committee was controlled by analytic philosophers.

Nothing better reveals the nutshell world in which many of them lived. Although the motives of some were unexceptionable, others were convinced that by this move they could squelch a small fringe group of troublemakers and whining paranoids. They had lost contact completely with philosophers still thinking in the older, historical styles—even those still attending the conventions—and, of course, with those who had years ago ceased coming to the conventions entirely. (And it was just the latter who, if they could be induced to pay their dues, would tend to vote pluralistically on a mail ballot!)

Even when such a ballot was instituted, and pluralistic candidates began doing very well, established analysts still could or would not see the palpable fact that an historical shift in the profession of philosophy might be proceeding behind their thin shell all around them. Thus the blindness of professionalism, bureaucracy, and the pure of mind.

But amendment of the constitution and adoption of the mail ballot would take time, and Christmas 1980 would see another election on the floor of a business meeting. This time, the meeting was in Boston, home of Harvard and MIT—"hard and real" philosophy. We asked Justus Buchler to be our candidate and he accepted. We regarded him as a redoubtable and creative speculative philosopher, well grounded in classical American philosophy. But illness (which turned out to be terminal) prevented him from continuing.

We then turned to William Barrett, veteran pluralist. Barrett is a venerable and graceful thinker, the mentor of Sherover and myself at NYU, the author of *Irrational Man*. But he had dared to mix academic philosophy with book reviewing in the *Atlantic,* and with notable articles in the highly regarded but nonprofessional *Partisan Review.* Barrett was unclean, and he had refused to shut his mouth and stay his hand. He had many enemies. I knew we could expect a backlash in Boston; we would probably lose, and I was painfully ambivalent about our nod to Barrett. I did not want to see him hurt.

My forebodings were soon realized. Grunbaum was renominated by the Nominating Committee. But three others were also nominated, including Barrett, for we had sent in many slips to the committee suggesting him, and they were not about to make the same mistake as last year.

In November, a letter had been circulated. It was without date or letterhead. It closed with "signed" and a list of typewritten names appeared. Each person named had been President of the Eastern Division fairly recently, beginning with Quine in 1957. Under the banner of maintaining "high professional standards" and resisting "factional pressures," the letter argued for support of Grunbaum for President and two other analytic philosophers for Executive Committee, in order to "counteract the effects of last year's election." What falls outside the criteria set by the self-anointed group is little better than riffraff.

> The Committee on Pluralism seeks to obtain, through political means, a position of influence which its members have not been able to obtain through their philosophical work. We believe that the Committee favors the suppression of serious scholarly and intellectual standards under the false banner of openmindedness.

One of those listed under "signed" was reported to have said that he never signed such a letter. No public statement of any kind was forthcoming from him, however. Quine is reported to have allowed that individual pluralists may have done some quality work, but that "he did not know their work."[3] No admission that his involvement with the letter might be the result of a moment's flippancy, pique, or inadvertence, was forthcoming, nor was any statement of regret or apology.

I myself was treated to a frigid letter from Quine. Its reasoning was so elaborate, condensed, and mathematical that I had great difficulty following it, though I read it several times. I am unable to judge the validity of his argument. Perhaps he intended to teach me—existentially, so to speak, or as a Zen master might—that I was incompetent.

Do not stir a fire with a knife, said Pythagoras. Do not affront the powerful and the arrogant. A corollary of the ahistorical manner in which the "signatories" of this letter had, with few exceptions, approached philosophy was to suggest to themselves and their students that they were the philosophers most worth studying in the thousands of years of philosophy. They referred to each others' work; they made each other famous within the tight world of professionalized philosophy. Their arrogance knew no bounds, and they deceived themselves by thinking that a few words of scorn for Pluralists, or perhaps an argument no one could follow, would be sufficient. As if all that was necessary was to cuff a bedraggled cur and it would slink away.

The conference in Boston was grim. Grunbaum was elected, Barrett was second. There were few reconciliations. But steps were taken, with our strong cooperation, to speed the adoption of a mail ballot. In addition to this important change in the constitution of the APA, an amendment was adopted which allowed any twenty-five members to nominate by petition any other member for any office. The ability of any analytic group to control the Nominating Committee through backroom procedures was sharply limited. With these changes, a new era became possible.

Since the adoption of the mail ballot in 1981, five more candidates whom we have supported have been elected to the Executive Committee, and three more presidents, Quentin Lauer and Joseph Kockelmans (both nominated by our petition), and Richard Bernstein. [Please recall that this essay was written in 1985 or 1986.] The new Secretary of the division was also supported by us. For the first time in decades, the Executive Committee is not openly antagonistic to Pluralistic exploration.

Most importantly, since the Program Committee is appointed by the Executive Committee, a broadening of the program is already evident. Many historical tendencies combine to reduce the hold of purists and self-appointed arbiters of philosophical competency, and given our continued attention to these matters, this loosening can be expected to continue. A whole generation of younger philosophers is the hope of the profession, a generation for whom the rigid formalisms and exclusions of positivism and analysis are secretly or openly boring, and for whom imagination, common sense, general education, and graciousness hold some allure.

Still, change is fairly slow, many philosophers do not take seriously the names of philosophers outside their own coterie: the closet of contemporaneity. Many will not yet acknowledge change, and I can only suppose that this is evidence for the thesis of my upcoming book, *The Moral Collapse of the University:*[4] An aversion to mixing and polluting occurs on a precritical, probably preconscious level of mind. Rather, it occurs on a precritical level of body-mind or body-self—the self in recoiling flight from itself.

As I've said, the preceding was written in 1985 or '86. What are the prospects for philosophy at the beginning of the new millennium?

Soon after I defended my dissertation in 1966, I was walking on the street one day in Washington Square with William Barrett. His voice shifted to another level, and I sensed that something that had been left unsaid for years was about to be said. Within this aura it surfaced—as if out of a rising globular skin of shining ocean water a great back would appear. "You know, Bruce, one can lose one's job for being a phenomenologist."

Luckily I got tenure early and still have a job. But after thirty-five years I have confirmed the truth of his statement. Faced with declining student enrollments and massive public indifference, academic philosophy has become increasingly technical, "analytic," defensive, insular, too often a Mandarin pastime. After our victory in 1978, Ruth Marcus, the logician who served as national president of the APA, was reported to have said, "You keep the conventions, we'll keep the graduate schools."

Such a canny strategy! She knew that apprentices in a tight job market would follow their masters. I was guardedly optimistic in 1985. I am less optimistic in 2001. The ethos of scientism is all-pervasive and nearly suffocating. Barrett had put his finger on the most salient trait of analytic philosophy: its disgust with, or dread of, phenomenology. As I've tried to show, this discipline seeks to further our most fundamental prescientific perceptions and intuitions, and thus allies it at crucial points with indigenous awareness. This is anathema to most analytic philosophers, for they strain to leave "the primitive past" behind. In the grip of the Enlightenment, they bet everything on formal logic; or on reasoning that uses high abstractions concerning "the mind" or "rights"; or on certain conceptions of science. In general they want to construct calculi which generate crudely verifiable results. Anything, anything except really looking, looking around, feeling, hearkening.

But as Black Elk put it, the Tree of the World that holds all things together may not be wholly dead.[5] Our need for regenerative thought and action is tremendously powerful: it is not easily pent up. Regeneration requires gratitude for the gifts of the world that come unbidden. If academic philosophy keeps turning narcissistically within itself, keeps turning away from what Emerson called the "Horizon," and Black Elk the "Hoop of the World," regenerative thinking on this level will break out in unlikely places. Already this is happening with certain cognitive scientists, for example, who see the potential for their science in William James's phenomenology! Bruce Mangan writes of the value of James's "mixed mode of investigation" ("Taking Phenomenology Seriously," cited earlier) and Bernard Baars uses James centrally in his *The Theatre of Consciousness: The Workspace of the Mind* (New York: Oxford, 1997).

The Tree of the World is sorely beleaguered but not dead. Dostoevsky described the human race as the ungrateful species. At least he believed it to be such within the Europe of the later nineteenth century. Perhaps we can learn to be less ungrateful? Learn to let the gifts of the world—what is given to be thought—inform our hearts and minds ecstatically?

It is hard to tell what is going to happen. Great changes sometimes come abruptly and when least expected.

Notes

1. I was surprised to see the article, but not greatly so. Ten days previously I had hand-carried a letter to the publisher of the *New York Times* detailing our activities. (I was stopped at the ground floor elevator by armed guards. I relinquished the letter only after one of them assured me he would deliver it. I assume it was delivered.) Perhaps it was a factor in dispatching a reporter.

2. The article did not report a strange moment of the previous night's meeting. It had been a stormy night in New York City. A window behind the rostrum had blown open, and had sent white curtains billowing out. John McDermott was speaking, and had muttered clearly enough for us at least to hear, "That was James entering the hall." Yes, nearly anything seemed to be possible that night.

3. "Analysts Win Battle in War of Philosophy," The *New York Times,* January 6, 1981, Edward B. Fiske.

4. Previously cited.

5. *Black Elk Speaks: Being the Life Story of a Holy Man of the Oglala Sioux As Told Through John Neihardt* (Lincoln: University of Nebraska Press, 1988 [1932]), p. 274.

4
Phenomenology in the United States

The roots of phenomenology in the United States are deep and complex. Let us begin with a broad notion of phenomenology: at the very least it means respect for things and events just as they appear. Phenomenology is the attempt to live and describe in service to the appearances, in service to the phenomena. This holds for all versions of phenomenology, from the strictly Husserlian forms to what has been called the existential.

This respect for things and events just as they appear, just as they grab us and demand to be described by us, is found in many of the Milesian pre-Socratic Greek thinkers. Heraclitus is famous for his gnomic sayings, one of which is, Nature loves to hide. Yes, but Heraclitus pursues Nature through the layers and outbacks of its *appearing;* he doesn't just suppose unperceivable entities that putatively explain appearances.

Likewise Plato: he is famous for his idea that transphenomenal Ideas discerned through the eye of the mind—not the body—are the underlying causes or structures of what appears. But he advises us to save the phenomena: that is, to so envision reality that we grasp things just as they appear. In still other words: that we do not get so carried away in *explaining* that we lose sight of just what it is that is to be *explained*—phenomena that must first be *described* if they are to be explained by the transphenomenal Ideas.

All phenomenologies of the last two hundred years can be loosely grouped together on this broad basis: they all stand opposed to reductionist tendencies in modern scientific-philosophical thought that continue reductionist movements in certain ancient Greek thinkers. I mean movements exemplified by Democritus, say, epitomized in the fragment, "By convention there is sweet, by convention bitter, but in reality there are only atoms and the void." The conventional phenomenal level is thought to be the superficial: it is more or less changeable and dependent upon hidden conditions that those caught up in it do not imagine. It is hardly real and we needn't bother, it seems, to describe it closely or to "save" it, as Plato wanted.

Nearly any version of phenomenology has great existential significance. If phenomena or appearances are not believed to be fully real and important, one's self can not be believed to be so either. For our sense of our value, weight, and power depends greatly on our immediate sense of how we affect the rest of the world, and it us. Also on how we resonate with the rest of the world. Impact and resonance make sense on a gut and immediate level only in terms of how things appear to us. That is, in terms of how arrayed phenomena press themselves upon us, and bend to and support, or obdurately resist, our efforts.

Let us further review the history of philosophy. Let us try to grasp how scientistic and reductionist tendencies to discount the phenomena have brought us to our present existential crisis and to widespread nihilism.

Descartes is aptly termed the father of modern philosophy. This is apt description, for he anticipated in paradigmatic ways the modern obsession—magnificent though some think it—with penetrating the "veil" of appearances and discovering the hidden or semihidden material causes of things. This is not immediately apparent because of Descartes's initial fix on mind and thought as the self-evident reality. But he believes that the veil of appearances or phenomena must be broken through, and can be so only by two drastic procedures which leave it tattered: he must through pure reason prove the existence of an all powerful, all-good, transcendent God who would not create beings who could not, to some degree, comprehend His underlying creation. This must be true at least when His creatures think in the very best way in which they have been endowed to think—that is, thinking as mechanistic-mathematical physicists. The basic realities are invisible and, in every sense, insensible atoms. But not this time in the void—as was the case with Democritus—but atoms composing extended bodies that form a plenum, a fullness of material reality, impinging within itself, that allows no void.

By the time of Immanuel Kant, alarm over reductionism and nihilism was spreading. Kant himself was a scientist in the mechanistic mode, and yet he saw that the experienced phenomenal world that formed the matrix of our distinctively human lives was being torn to pieces. If the only reliable realities are what is described in mechanistic-mathematical physics—realities "underlying" the phenomena—then our experiences of goodness and beauty are undervalued, relegated to the closet of the merely conventional, the contingently conditioned and unreliable, the merely apparent.

Hence Kant's massive efforts to save the phenomena and also our distinctively human experiences, values, motivations—our civilizations. I will not rehearse this here, aside from noting that he found something irreducible and evident in human will and freedom; also in our ability to make judgments concerning ends and purposes that are not reducible to judgments about the mechanical conditions that supposedly cause and explain the present and the future in terms of the past.

And we can, according to Kant, appreciate the world as that which certainly *appears* to possess purposiveness though we can't specify just what the purpose is. We are caught up in a beautiful, sublime, mysterious world in which directly experienced appreciations and obligations are as real as anything imaginable. The distinctively human needn't go down the drain.

To say that Kant massively influenced the ensuing two hundred years, and was a bulwark for many philosophers in resisting crass material-ism, reductionism, and demoralization, is to say what should be obvious. But his ingenious and far-ranging salvaging effort depended on a funda-mental distinction that later phenomenologists either rejected or greatly modified.

As is well known, Kant divided reality into two realms: what appears to us, the phenomenal, and what never could, the noumenal. Schelling's and Hegel's greatly ambitious phenomenologies-metaphysics reject this fundamental distinction. In this brief introduction to phenomenology in the United States I will mention only Hegel (though it is Schelling who most crucially influenced the later phenomenologies of Charles Peirce and Martin Heidegger).

In his famous *Phenomenology of Spirit* (or *Mind*), Hegel objected to the visual metaphor that molds Kant's thinking. It's as if Descartes and then Kant thought that the mind was a kind of lens that lies between us and an external world (again the idea of a veil, though translucent, which separates us from the world—a veil as the *merely* apparent). If we ascertain the limits and the distortions of the lens we can subtract these out of our account of reality, correct for them, and get some idea, however limited (as in Kant's case), of what is "out there."

This fundamentally begs the question of reality, thinks Hegel. For the idea of the lens as a metaphor for the mind (and for appearances "in the mind") presupposes that there is something *beyond the lens,* in the "external world," that gets refracted through it! Descartes's attempt to doubt the existence of the external world is phony, a "paper doubt" as Peirce puts it, and his arguments for a God who guarantees our best knowledge are specious. With his distinction between phenomena and noumena, Kant too is caught up in a kind of speciousness, Hegel thinks, though Kant rejects Descartes's arguments for God.

Hegel's metaphysics requires his phenomenology. He concentrates on what "immediately gives itself out," the phenomenon. It's a mere *that,* meaning merely "something there," but no *what:* we know yet nothing of what the thing or event is itself. And with this version of phenomenology Hegel can set his immense metaphysics in motion. We begin with brute Being, but it is also Nothing (it has no essence or whatness). And so, given a dialectic of Being and Nothing, we get Becoming, in terms of which all history—intellectual, spiritual, economical, political, physical—can be understood as what it is. Apparently, we find in Hegel the most completely nonreductive account of reality possible.

But subsequent phenomenologists from Peirce and James through Husserl, Heidegger, Merleau-Ponty, and still others in the United States, will not buy Hegel's version of phenomenology. It is reductivist, though in an odd way: it reduces the experienced world to the workings of a dialectical logic discerned, or fabricated, by a version of pure reason. Kant's idea of a critique of pure reason must be taken up again, this time with phenomenologies purged of Descartes's and then Hegel's ratiocinative and mentalistic biases ("thinking God's thoughts after Him"—do tell!).

Charles Peirce early tried to come up with a long list of ontological categories reminiscent of Hegel's in *Encyclopaedia of the Philosophical Sciences.* He gave it up, mainly because he could not generate the categories in Hegelian fashion as a phenomenology that spins a metaphysics out of itself dialectically. Peirce, James, and Husserl are all suspicious of brute *thats* that are encysted in pure Being, the first step in the Hegelian dialectical unwrapping of the world. For Peirce, James, Husserl, there *are* thats: Peirce's category of secondness is there to accommodate them; for example, the experience we get when we run into a post blindfolded. For James there are thats—"though ready to become all kinds of whats."

But unlike Hegel, none of them equate the immediately given *that* with pure Being: it's not a *brute* that. It's a moment in our experiencing, true, but not a dialectical "moment" in the inexorable career of an Absolute Mind. If we are really good phenomenologists we will see that the *that* moments are themselves pregnant with possibility, and this includes the possibility at least of a context, of a world-experienced by us. James saw, as I said, that the thats are ready to become all kinds of whats.[1]

We should take the "all kinds" seriously. When we take the critique of pure reason to heart, we see that there is no single dialectical path within an Absolute Mind marked out before us. We see that there are an indefinite number of ways of sizing up and constituting a world in our experience. The *thats* ready to become all kinds of *whats* open out onto our situations. These in turn open out onto horizons of possible modes of being that are presented as unimaginable in their specifics. But they are presented as pregnant with a world-to-be-experienced-by-us.

Indeed, the phenomenon of the unimaginable "beyond the horizon" can itself be described just as it presents itself—and must be if we are not to be arrogant fools. Meaning is a matter of things' experienceability, and this must be pushed to include what is imagined as not-actually-experienceable-by-us. (This is an imagining, but the imagined is presented as "plausible enough!") The meaning of "world" must include "the mysterious."

For Peirce and James, pure reason—even if it be the Hegelian dialectical variety—can supply no substitute for the world's concrete richness, openness, mysteriousness. Peirce is himself a great systematizer, but not in the Hegelian manner. For Peirce—mathematician, logician, chemist, physicist, geographer—the prerequisite of all intellectual work is mathematics. Philosophy proper begins with what he calls phaneroscopy: from the Greek *phaneron,* or phenomenon, that which is to be described in its primal or immediate givenness.

Now, it might seem that placing mathematics first would pollute the phenomenon in its immediacy. But Peirce is a greatly creative mathematician. The model of arithmetic does not dominate his mathematics; that is, Peirce is not exclusively concerned with the units we form in order to do arithmetical calculations. He is also caught up in the theoretical mathematics of the continuum. This he defines as an extent or stretch of any sort that cannot be constructed or constituted out of any set of discrete units or any stages.

Immediately, in his mathematics, Peirce has guarded himself against premature crystalization or individuation. He is in position to oppose the whole Cartesian and British empiricist tradition which supposes discrete and individual mental entities such as "sense data." And what does Hegel—or anybody—mean by *a that!* It is an artificial, a misplacedly arithmetical, "cut out" (though perhaps essential for practical life). And to discover it in pure Being? It is simply the point of immediate stress in a whole system of means and meanings, the whole world as experienced or experienceable by us, no matter how occluded this world may be at moments, and no matter how inchoate and ill-defined at others.

The phenomenological structures in Peirce are forgotten at our peril. We must remind ourselves of them at times, because he is also a great logician, a fine mathematician and philosopher of science, and a working scientist. But he never forgot that Logic is concerned with representations, not presentations; it is not phenomenology. Its normativity should not be projected mindlessly into phenomenology.[2] His triune set of categories and his vast theory of signs will compose what he probably thought of as "the master science, the glue that [he hoped] would re-cement the broken soul of Western civilization. It will reunite the split . . . between matter and mind, between nature and spirit, physics and psychics . . . natural science and the humanities."[3]

Though James differs from Peirce in crucial respects, he is thoroughly aligned with him on the fundamental importance of phenomenology. Although he never, I believe, ascribes the word to his own work, he is in fact eminently phenomenological at pivotal points in his world-view.[4] He is greatly suspicious of any attempts to reduce and devalue the immediately experienced, the phenomenon. To think there are causes "hidden in the cubic deeps" that explain causation as immediately experienced and exercised in the world, is to beg the fundamental question. It is to model our causal principle after the immediately experienced phenomenon of causation, and then to forget what we've modelled it after![5] That is, it is to forget causation as an immediately experienced phenomenon inherent in our bodily existence. And with this we lose touch with ourselves.

James's ability to grasp the immediately perceived world just as it is perceived "hot off the griddle of the world," goes hand in hand with his abilities as an artist. And also with his ability—an ethical ability, I believe—to empathize with the many and various forms of living, and with the many and various forms of happening and knowing. He could let things be in their sometimes shocking immediacy. He tells us, for example, that an artist painting the heavy shade of a tree on a bright day will not simply darken the shaded area, but will really look to see how the shade really looks in these present and actual conditions. When it looks purple, he uses purple to paint it.[6] As to his ethical abilities to grasp humans in their humanity, no matter how odd we may find them, see his "On a Certain Blindness in Human Beings." It is a monument to empathy.

Always James fixes on meaning, and the various meanings of meaning. In this he heavily influenced Husserl in the 1890s. Anticipating Husserl's *epoche* or abstention, James notes that to get at meaning we must interrupt the habits that structure our daily practice, habits that are crusts that separate us from the freshets and springs of meaning-making. He guards the juice and sap of phenomena, and the juice and sap of ourselves.

To get at meaning, James counsels us to pump free air around things. As I said, this anticipates Husserl. To allow meaning to billow out, Husserl, with his notion of *epoche,* counsels us to abstain from *simply* asserting something's existence. But rather to assert it "within the phenomenological bracket." That is, to assert, for example, that something certainly appears to exist, and we do not doubt that *appearance* at all. With this the full meaning of existence has a chance to billow out and display itself. (As Dewey says later in "Philosophy and Civilization," "Meaning is prior to, and more precious than, [empirical] truth.") The multiple aspects of the actual world *as meant* can burgeon, billow out: the richness and orientation of the immediately experienced phenomenal world shown to be the essential matter that it is. Phenomenology is a deep root of existentialism.

The routinizations and pressures of everyday living force meaning into a straight jacket. James uses the example of smelling violets. The world seems to say, "Well, get on with it, describe it, we don't have all day. It's violets you're smelling, not roses or magnolias, right?" So we name the experience of smelling "after its thing," James says. But the experiencing really discloses "a thousand things," the whole system or context of properties and associations in which the experienced violets are embedded. The experiencing should be named after them all, but that is impossible practically. Still, we can abstain from simply asserting, "The violets exist and are the proximate cause of my experiencing them." When we do, the meaning of those things, and of ourselves, is free to billow out. (See my *William James and Phenomenology,* indexed under, "the psychologist's fallacy.")

Husserl credits James's *Principles of Psychology* (1890) with helping him find his way out of psychologism.[7] That once popular—at times recurrent—"ism" held that since everything thought about is thought about in a thinking, and since psychology is the science of psychical processes such as thinking, the ultimate science is psychology. The fallacy springs from failing to realize how utterly fundamental to thinking and meaning is the world immediately thought about or meant. The fallacy springs from a residual, fragmentary Cartesianism which pictures mind as an internal domain. No, mind is radically open, it is organisms' minding of a world minded. If what is thought about is mathematical, mathematics must be used to deliver the meaning; if geological, then geology; if grammatical, then grammar; if logical, then logic; if cosmical or religious, then religious experience as its own discipline, and so forth.

Husserl also credits James with the idea of horizon (which James often names "fringe").[8] That is, elements experienced in any way are never experienced as isolated, as we just saw, but as multiply related to other things, as beings-in-the-world, as beings-in-the-world-along-with-us!

We must now look at Husserl's grand project for meaning retention and meaning releasement, his transcendental phenomenology. We must if we would understand phenomenology after Husserl, particularly in the United States. As Hegel had a love-hate relationship with Descartes (Hegel thinks that with him subjectivity sails toward its port, starts at least to come home to itself), so did Husserl. After all, Husserl did write *Cartesian Meditations* rather late in his career.

Of course, Descartes the philosopher-scientist doesn't properly appreciate the primacy of meaning over empirical fact, according to Husserl. Descartes thinks that once the factual reality of the external world is established, by establishing the existence of a good creator-God, then the thinking ego is a "tag end" of this factual world: so Husserl critiques Descartes.[9] Husserl believes that the rennaissance French thinker doesn't grasp that the ego basic to philosophy cannot be an individual human's empirical ego; it must be the transcendental ego. That is, it must be the intersubjective reality in which, and only in which, humanity can do anything that it does, for example, doubt the existence of the material world, or prove it, or think or do anything.

Husserl is responding to the crisis of meaning and of civilization that so many discerned at the end of the eighteenth century, for the prime example, Kant. If we think that the only reliable sciences are the empirical sciences of the time, we will fail to shore up our lives, everything will unravel in nihilism and meaninglessness. All empirical sciences depend upon a matrix of prescientific meanings. Husserl thought that we need a "strict science" of meanings which would thematize and protect this matrix.

Hence his transcendental phenomenology with its transcendental ego. Within the intersubjectivity of humanity all meanings are constituted, and because *meanings* are constituted, they connect with other meanings in a way that mere factual events never could—events that we could imagine at least to be other than they are. Meanings connect to meanings essentially, necessarily, in a way that we cannot imagine could be other than they are, and the connections form necessary truths discovered by the strict science of phenomenology. For example, in the very meaning of "actual thing perceived" inheres the further meaning "cannot be fully grasped in any experience or series of experiences." So, in the statement, "Actual things cannot be fully grasped in any experience or series of experiences," the meaning of the predicate is contained in the meaning of the subject. So the statement is necessarily true. As James put it earlier (before the advent of Husserl's stringent method and without Husserl's mathematicism) existing reality is perceived as voluminous, as overflowing all that we can say, think, or do about it. And we can think *that*.

If all connections of meanings are self-evidently true when the transcendental ego is displayed, then Husserl proposed that all the presuppositions of this position must themselves be made self-evident. He looked for a domain of absolute consciousness, self-sufficient and absolutely impregnable by any form of skepticism. Civilization itself requires this, he thought. Husserl was led to a kind of idealism, it seems: reality is basically mind or consciousness. All cognition is fundamentally of essences—correlates of consciousness—and particular things are mere instances of essences.

Hermeneutical or existential phenomenologists, whether American or European, reject the strict science features of Husserl's phenomenology. All contingent features of our experiencing of the world cannot be removed, they think. As Merleau-Ponty put it in the introduction to his *Phenomenology of Perception,* the main discovery of Husserl's program of "reduction to essences" is that the reduction can never be complete. There is always something left over, unreduced, wild, contingent, or as yet undiscovered. Indeed, the very decision to engage in Husserlian phenomenology is rife with our freedom and finitude, with our existence. The decision itself cannot be placed within a matrix of self-evidence. It involves factors that we probably cannot imagine.

Phenomenologists in the United States can first be characterized in terms of their relationship to Husserl, although, of course, their position relative to the whole history of philosophy must be considered too. I will give special attention to one of these, James Edie. It is not just Edie's contributions in founding the Society for Phenomenology and Existential Philosophy (SPEP), that has done so much to keep phenomenology alive in the United States: without his work SPEP would not exist. Nor is it his

formidable sheaf of weighty articles and books on broad-ranging phenomenological methods and topics that affords him pride of place. It is also
because—perhaps uniquely, I believe—his work embodies both Husserlian and existential-phenomenological elements. He is pivotal for understanding phenomenology in the United States into the twenty-first
century.

As we will see, James Edie believes that there are necessary truths to
be discerned phenomenologically, and without which we slip into nihilism. But he also sees the immense role that contingency, ignorance, impulse, decision play in human life. From this derives his love of the arts—
particularly theatre—in their ability to point up, to at least partially il-
luminate, our pressing and at times gruelling situations. Derived also is his
belief that choices must be made without benefit of a full complement of
essential truths or reasons. One might say Edie embodies in one thinker
both Husserl and Jean-Paul Sartre, as well as William James, and exhibits
what I take to be a trait generally of United States phenomenology: it is
more historically rooted than some main incarnations of its Continental
cousin, and, I want to say, it is more balanced than is its cousin.

After Edie, I will consider (inevitably in shorter compass) John Wild,
Aron Gurwitsch, William Barrett, Calvin Schrag, important phenomenologists who occupied professorships in major North American
universities. Inevitably, given the format, I must limit my examination to
this group. Certain others quickly come to mind, William Earle, Hubert
Dreyfus, Edward Casey, John Sallis, Charles Scott, Don Ihde . . .

My first and my last meetings with Jim Edie remain vivid. In 1968, I
believe, at some convention, I first encountered the Edie presence: the
intent eyes, the subdued voice, the fast walk. Bert Dreyfus had told him
about my dissertation on James's *The Principles of Psychology* as a phenomenological investigation. Edie had stayed up and missed some meetings to
read it; and he really liked it, his whole presence told me. (My adviser,
William Barrett, was delighted when I told him. "Edie doesn't like anything!") Edie's endorsement greatly buoyed me. Which I needed, because
most of my fellow graduate students had dismissed James as a lightweight.

My last meeting with Jim in January of 1998 a few weeks before he
died revealed a greatly changed man. About five years earlier he had had
cancerous portions of tissue cut out of his throat, tongue, and shoulder. He
walked slowly, listing slightly to the left, and while he had trained himself
to talk with the tip of his tongue missing, he spoke with some difficulty. In
the last five years of his life, eating had been greatly difficult, for most of his

saliva glands were gone, and he used cold wine or iced milk to wash down the food, wincing all the time. Greatly changed he was, and yet his determination, his psychical mobilization, was as apparent as ever; indeed, he was an exemplar of industry and courage.

There's a tragic dimension to Jim's life which extends beyond the collapse of his health. Indeed, it extends beyond his individual career as a philosopher. Let's look at academic philosophy in the United States since about 1930, particularly as this affected philosophers not willing to stay confined within so-called analytic philosophy. You may recall that the phenomenologists Alfred Schutz and Aron Gurwitsch, fleeing from Hitler, had found a haven at the New School for Social Research in Manhattan. They formed the reasonable-sounding plan to establish contact with American philosophers by writing of William James's phenomenological work and how it influenced Husserl.

But they were badly out of touch with the American academic-philosophical scene at that time, the 1930s and '40s. The great "classical" American philosophers' reputations were at their lowest ebb at just this time. They had been pushed from the limelight by the newest imports from England and the Continent: positivism along with a slew of "analyses" (psychoanalysis, ordinary language, social-marxist analysis, etc.). Though Dewey still lived, and though two of my teachers—Sidney Hook and William Barrett—vividly represented pragmatism and existential-phenomenology, these ways of thinking had passed out of favor with philosophical power brokers in the APA.

When Jim Edie first appeared on the scene in the early 1960s, things looked like they might shift. Gurwitsch published his *Theorie du Champ de la Conscience* in 1957 and Johannes Linschoten his *Auf dem Wege zu Einer Phänomenologischen Psychologie: Die Psychologie von William James* in 1961 (Dutch original 1959). Both were excellent books that linked James closely to the development of modern phenomenology and established Husserl's indebtedness to James, and both were fairly soon translated into English.

Also a few native-born American philosophers tried to reestablish contact between the classical American thinkers, particularly James, and their Continental brethren. John Wild at Harvard had been developing a realistic or existential phenomenology and found James an ally waiting for him. Wild's *The Radical Empiricism of William James* appeared in 1969. Barrett I've already mentioned. My own dissertation was published in 1968.

Edie was a dynamo in the '60s, galvanizing all kinds of publications and activities that seemed might reinvigorate an American phenomenology. As I said, he was a founder of SPEP. He also served on the executive board of the International Association for Philosophy and Literature, an exuberant group founded by Hugh Silverman. Edie's writings on James were both solid and imaginative. For notable examples, see "The Genesis of a Phenomenological Theory of the Experience of Personal Identity: William James on Consciousness and the Self" (1973), and "Notes on the Philosophical Anthropology of William James" (anthologized in 1965). These and other clear and marvelous essays were collected in his *William James and Phenomenology* in the mid-1980s.

Jim told me a year before his death that he thought that this book had had at best a few dozen readers. As Gurwitsch and Schutz had been wrong in the 1930s about America's readiness to keep developing our own phenomenology, so Edie, Wild, Barrett, myself, and some others were wrong in the '60s and '70s. Some interest in Continental philosophy—as it was called—remained or emerged, alright, but what an interest! Before we knew it, Hegel was being reexamined (in books by John Findlay and Charles Taylor). It was Hegel's tortured version of phenomenology that captured some attention.

As if to prove Hegel himself right in his dialectical reasoning, interest had jumped as far as possible from positivism and scientism toward their apparent opposite, leapfrogging completely over Husserl, James, Heidegger, Merleau-Ponty, Wild, Edie, et cetera! Back to Hegel.

But that wasn't all. Contemporary Continental philosophy in sometimes blatantly anti-phenomenological garb popped up in America from across the water: the Frankfurt schools and various and sundry Parisian schools. Some of this was interesting and substantial work (e.g., some Foucault, Habermas, Irigary). Much else, however, was slightly hysterical, or nihilistic, or narcissistic; so it seemed to me and to some others, including Edie. In any case, Husserl's hope to stave off nihilism by locating all special studies—whether scientific, literary, or historical—in a thematized and honored matrix of prescientific phenomena and meanings was short-circuited, forgotten, or ridiculed.

Edie's work in particular had staked out a region that could have proven a staging area for integrating inquiries and reweaving a matrix for thought and life. To mention a few of the salients: In *Speaking and Meaning: The Phenomenology of Language* (Bloomington: Indiana University Press, 1976), Edie pointed out how Husserl's phenomenology could connect with Noam Chomsky's idea of depth grammar and rid it at once both of its Cartesian folklore and its psychologistic and biologistic accessories.

> If . . . it is possible to interpret the "formal universals" of language which constitute the base rules of deep grammar as aprioris in Husserl's sense, then we can easily separate the essence of Chomsky's work from the Cartesian folklore in which it is imbedded. . . . Since apriori grammatical constraints on the meaningfulness of sentences belong to the first level of formal logic, . . . they are constraints on understanding as such and that, if there be intelligent life on some planet other than Earth, or in the "spiritual creatures" of medieval theology, then, in principle, it would be possible for us to learn their languages and communicate with them. What divides Husserl and Chomsky, then, is whether the universals of grammar are to be understood in a genetically biological (and thus necessarily psychologistic) sense, or whether they are to be understood in terms of the logical transcendentalism of Kantian and Husserlian phenomenology. . . . This kind of distinction between surface and depth grammar is exactly what Husserl was aiming at when he distinguished "the grammatical" from empirical grammar, though he nowhere anticipated the spectacular developments in linguistic theory which Chomsky has initiated without him. (p. 59 ff)

Communications with conscious and intelligent beings anywhere presuppose a shared depth grammar, no matter how different on certain levels their languages might be. Or, though we may believe two contradictory statements at once, all cultures believe, Edie believes, that both cannot *be* true. There is self-evident insight into the formal and a priori structures of reason itself.[10] Differently put, not all points are amendable or positions revisable through conversation (a term much used by Richard Rorty, for example), since for conversation itself to be possible, certain conditions must be met, and a select group of truths must hold. This is the Husserlian strand; but, notice, it is a necessary condition for sane human thought and action, Edie thinks, not a sufficient.

Nobody I know of has followed up on Edie's bridging work. Hence we are left, in *au courent* analytic "philosophy of mind," with Cartesian folklore and various biologisms and psychologisms. I mean, for example, easy assumptions made in psycholinguistics about inborn concepts, or about "representations and tokens in the head." I mean general alienation from our situatedness as minding, intensionally informed bodies that can be caught up ecstatically and preverbally in the world around us. I mean naive Cartesian assumptions about "the internal" and "the external" clogging apparently brilliant and critical work in philosophy of mind. It all *looks* scientific. In reality it is scientism out of touch with the actual work of science in our century. I think again of physicist John Wheeler's remark, "There's no *out there* out there." I think he means that reality is a sea of energy exchange between nodes within the sea, and what we call mind is but one aspect of the exchange, another aspect of which we call matter.

Other salients of Edie's work that might yet serve an integrative and bridging function go inadequately tended. Most obviously, his work on William James has not been followed up by professional philosophers, even those who advertise themselves as Americanists. In 1837, Emerson issued a declaration of intellectual independence in the clarion opening pages of "The American Scholar":

> Our day of dependence, our long apprenticeship to the learning of other lands, draws to a close. The millions that around us are rushing into life, cannot always be fed on the sere remains of foreign harvests. Events, actions arise, that must be sung, that will sing themselves.

But we find it hard to let things sing, and it is easier to declare independence than to achieve it. In fact, at the end of the twentieth century and the beginning of the twenty-first, professional American philosophy is burdened with unexamined baggage from foreign lands. I don't mean just Descartes. I mean the whole British empiricist as well as behaviorist and positivistic traditions—the legacy of atomism, disintegration, alienation. James's radical empiricism, which holds that relations are equiprimordial with things related, is not generally understood. Nor is his idea of pure experience: the level of primal prereflective involvement in the world prior to the very distinction between subject and object. Hilary Putnam is an exception in the trend. His "direct realism" is indebted to James.

Construing James as an existential phenomenologist—to which Edie contributed so much—opens up this primal domain of interfusion of sensient organism and the rest of the world. More, it affords contact with ancient indigenous traditions of shamanic perceiving and healing.

If we only look, the bridges ramify: radical empiricism, phenomenology, linguistics, current physics, indigenous American traditions of thought, belief, and action! Like so much else of Edie's work, the follow up is exceedingly slow in coming. This is lamentable, probably disastrous: for the fracture of European mentality from indigenous traditions, for example, is gravely hurtful to both. When shamanic healing works, it must be that the very reality of paradigmatically regenerative creatures—snakes and bears for example—irradiates and suffuses the bodies of patients.

In line with various field theories of twentieth century physics, James's pure experience predicts just this. There is no Cartesian veil of representations "in the mind" that divides us from the animals or plants *out there*. There is "no out there out there." The reality of animals and plants is not confined within the envelope of their surfaces. Rather, shells of energy, some specifiable some not, spread their being fieldlike to permeate our own, if we let them, if we don't clutch up in panic. The regenerative universe can flow through and enliven our own immune systems. An acute phenomenology is at least the first step in this process of discovery. Aroma therapy, for example, is not the ridiculous thing it might first appear to be.

We should not leave the topic of how Edie's work was dropped, untended, without mentioning his work in theatre. Perhaps I display my ignorance, but it seems to me that despite poststructuralist forays that giddily cross the line between fact and fiction, there is little solid work on the phenomenology of theatre. Jim pondered the significance of James's idea in *The Principles* of the social self: there are as many different selves of this sort as there are ideas of us in onlookers or interlocutors. How do our identities get built up, in great part, through the subtle and open-ended dialectics of our interpersonal exchanges? And most specifically, how does the experimentation on, and thematization of, these exchanges which theatre makes possible bring to light factors of interpersonal and personal reality not detectable otherwise?

Jim's approach to theatre was more along the James-Husserl-Sartre axis, and mine along the James-Heidegger one. We didn't talk at all about our concurrent work on the theatre. This adds its own little note to the tragic tenor of his career in philosophy.

When I saw him a few weeks before his death, we talked almost exclusively about the most practical matters, for instance, how to arrange for TIAA-CREF to get what remained of his retirement funds to his wife as quickly as possible after his demise. His large library had already been sold to a local Sarasota, Florida, bookseller, many of the volumes in Latin from his days as a seminarian in Rome. On her own, his wife had saved out single instances of the Northwestern phenomenology series which had done so much to keep a flame burning. I don't recall seeing books from the Indiana University Press series. Though I angered him slightly by going to his off-prints stored away and extracting single instances, I did do this, and will provide copies if interested persons contact me.

He both wanted me with him and did not want this. He did not like me seeing his dilapidated condition, but for about an hour a day he seemed to like to hear me talk. He fed himself now with liquid nutriments which he poured through a tube directly into his stomach. Only once did he show a wan smile when I spoke of anything explicitly philosophical: when I mentioned Jacques Derrida and his many followers. Fame and fortune seemed particularly meaningless in those hours with him.

I spoke to him in passing of very recent work by Bruce Mangan and Bernard Baars linking James's phenomenological psychology with the latest cognitive science.[11] He gave no response.

He faced a dreadful choice: Have his whole tongue removed on the chance that all the cancer would be eliminated, but entailing the complete loss of his powers of speech, or keep his tongue and his powers of speech, even though diminished, for as long as possible.

There were no necessary connections of meanings forming necessary, apodictic, or a priori truths that could help him decide. No such truths about human nature or goodness or obligation that could entail for this particular human being what the good thing to do surely was. He was locked into the domain of contingency, finitude, and anguish. And though we conversed, and so had to conform to certain conditions necessary for conversation itself, I could not help him.

Jim Edie had to freely create value, with no guarantee of the correctness of his choice. He chose to keep his tongue, to be an exemplar of the value of speech, even if it meant the immanent loss of his life. His last words to me a month before he died were, as he sank into bed, "I don't know what to do." But whether he *knew* or not, he chose resolutely; he created value.

One of John Wild's distinctions is that he is the first full professor to leave Harvard's philosophy department, the ancestral home of American philosophy, for another university. He was clearly discontented with the state of the department in 1961. Analytic philosophy ranked high. William Ernest Hocking (a student of James early influenced by Husserl) was retired.[12] C. I. Lewis was a link to the great past, and his influence was still felt, but he had adopted positions antithetical to Wild's. For example, Lewis held that the immediate givens in consciousness were sense data, neither true nor false, that were worked up by mind. He had abandoned

James's idea of knowledge by acquaintance, our immediate involvement with the world *as* world. And had abandoned James's (and Dewey's) view that sense-data are not primal building blocks of knowledge, but are derivative of analyses forgetful of themselves. All this struck Wild, a passionate and engaged being, as deracinated intellectualism.

If ever a philosopher was in search of roots, it was John Wild. Cartesianism was completely out for him. He early concentrated on the history of philosophy: Plato, in some of his aspects, Aristotle, Aquinas, Spinoza, for example. Anything suggesting idealism spoke to him of deracination, absence of involvement, loss of juice and sap; it was anathema to Wild. He founded the American Association for Realistic Philosophy in 1953.[13] We should not be surprised that he rejected Husserl's Transcendental Ego and Transcendental Idealism. Only Husserl's notion of the life-world interested him.

In 1955 he published *The Challenge of Existentialism,* (Bloomington: Indiana University Press) which became a philosophical best-seller. In a trip to Europe in 1957 he was inspired by Merleau-Ponty, and also gained a new appreciation of Heidegger's *Being and Time.* He was converted, some said, to existential phenomenology and existentialism. Fairly soon he left Harvard and took up the chairmanship of the philosophy department at Northwestern. Though he was there only a short time, before returning East to Yale, it was long enough to stir SPEP into being. Along with, of course, the young James Edie, and others including William Earle, Calvin Schrag, George Schrader, and the very young Edward Casey.

It is not surprising that Wild's search for roots led him to the version of existential phenomenology at which he arrived. He vehemently opposed the intellectualism, nominalism, and conventionalism he saw all around him. We are bodily beings with many needs, and on different levels. Goodness is a matter of deep vitality, it is not just a matter of what we happen to think is good, given our time and place. We might think wrongly. Our need for meaning is so strong that it can, on occasion, override our need for life itself. Yet we also have other needs, those inherited from an immemorial past in nature and culture.

As I understand Wild's notion of the challenge of existentialism, it is this: Following Kierkegaard, Heidegger, and James, we humans are distinguished by our ability to create possibility. When the possibility of possibility dawns for us, as Kierkegaard discerned, a quantum leap of change enters the world. In a real sense, possibility is prior to actuality, as Heidegger put it, and for James, the first act of freedom is the belief in freedom itself, the leap of affirmation. (Note that this also holds for Henry Bugbee, Essay 7.)

And yet we are also factical and contingent beings, thrown into situations and into habitual ways of behaving, into ways of life we did not design and did not initially choose to enter. How do we square the fact of our freedom and the fact of our facticity? How act so as not to go out of touch with our bodies, largely genetically but also culturally structured? What meaning is most meaningful? What meaning leads us into blind alleys or hopeless tangents? What meaning is worth dying for, if that terrible choice is presented us? We create ourselves, but not like God, *ex nihilo.*

The idea of ethical or existential choice as sheer arbitrariness disgusted Wild. There are what he calls facts of tendency, tendency in development and growth.[14] Goodness is a matter of fulfilling these tendencies; it is a matter of fulfillment and vitality. And there is also the fact of our freedom. The question is Socrates'—how to decide and act wisely? But now it is raised in a world without tried and true rites of passage and development, or generally accepted eternal verities. The challenge for us is awesome.

It is understandable that Wild's intellectual life would culminate in his last book, *The Radical Empiricism of William James* (New York: Doubleday and Co.) 1969. The fathers of distinctly American phenomenology are most plausibly James, along with Peirce. James's mode of phenomenology most keenly discerns our immediate involvements in the world around and through us. He discerns the tendencies and structures that make all our other experience possible—but without the transcendental apparatus, whether Kantian, Hegelian, or Husserlian. James's last projects are these: his radical empiricism—a level of immediate experience anterior to the very distinction between subject and object. And his vision of a pluralistic universe—endless variety, myriad forms of connectedness, the pleni-potential of our lives. James's work is unfinished, pregnant with possibilities. As Wild knew, these awaited us at the end of our century and the beginning of a new millennium.

Aron Gurwitsch was almost the exact contemporary of John Wild. In nearly every other respect they differed greatly: in national background, in temperament, in their attitudes toward Husserl. Yet Gurwitsch early joined forces with Wild in developing SPEP. The tension between the more

Husserlian form of phenomenology that Gurwitsch embodied and the existential form embodied by Wild was, on the whole, productive.

Wild and Gurwitsch did agree on the seminal importance of James, and we will see that Gurwitsch is as much influenced by James as by Husserl. In his chief published work, *The Field of Consciousness,* Gurwitsch attacked the notion of sense-data, thereby criticizing the residuum of that notion embedded in Husserl's idea of the material (*hyle*) of consciousness that gets worked up through rays of intentionality (*Ichstrahlen*) from the ego-subject. (In fact, Gurwitsch returns to Husserl's *Logical Investigations* of 1900, which is a non-egological approach to experience.)

As I have repeatedly emphasized, detailed critique of sense-data is a fundamental point of leverage for moving philosophy in new and more fruitful and relevant directions. Fundamental to Gurwitsch's critique is his attack on the "constancy hypothesis:" the thesis "that sense-data depend exclusively and exhaustively upon external stimuli, so that the same sensations recur whenever the same stimuli act upon the receptor organs."[15] In other words, Gurwitsch is refusing to describe perceptual experience as composed of irreducible constants and units (stimuli-sensations) which then get modified as a result of "internal conditions" or a "concept" or an "interpretation" of a nonperceptual or nonsensory sort.[16]

Gurwitsch's critique has the broadest ramifications. Recall the introduction to this essay in which I contrasted the ages-old genius of phenomenology—the demand that we describe exactly what appears just as it appears—to reductionist positions that prematurely posit a nonperceivable entity as the cause of the appearance. The appearance is prejudged, misdescribed, devalued as a mere epiphenomenon of, or dangler from, the so-called world of real causation beyond direct perception.

Irony of ironies, this atomism has now smuggled itself into the putative description of consciousness itself, what's immediately given in consciousness, sense-data—these fictional units, stimuli-sensations. If we really look, really discern what's given in the perceptual field, we will see that the constancy between stimulus and sensation cannot be made evident: it is an interpolation. And one that is not in principle falsifiable, for if no constancy between stimulus and sensation is evident, the lack of it can be referred to some as yet undetected "internal condition" or "subtly acting concept."

Recall how Charles Peirce placed mathematics at the head of all intellectual work. But it was an exceedingly subtle mathematics in which the idea of continuum was a structural member. That is, the idea that no set of units, no matter how subtle, or fine, or obvious, can compose a continuum. Peirce applies this idea throughout his philosophical account of reality, with phenomenology at the head of philosophy. We should be suspicious of all units, particularly those that show up in putative descriptions of the experienced world, and which cannot, in principle, be falsified. Such descriptions distort our own experience, our own living in our own lived world moment by moment.

Note as well that James already in 1890, in *The Principles of Psychology*, had anticipated the gist of Gurwitsch's critique of the constancy hypothesis. He described it as "the psychologist's fallacy."[17] That is, instead of describing the phenomenon just as it appears, the "natural scientific" psychologist describes it in terms of what he or she believes causes it, thereby committing a violation of the priority of description over scientific-causal explanation. For example, as we have seen, instead of describing the sight and smell of violets just as these are perceived, in all their amplitude and halo of relations, we say merely "sight and smell of violets."

That is, we describe the experienced world in terms of what we believe causes the experience, the violets "out there." If we thought for a moment we would see that this is absurdly truncated *even* as a causal explanation: in fact, what is involved is a vast feed-out, feed-back loop of causal interactivity of organism in environment.

But we have been trained, in effect, not to think, and not to observe really closely. So we describe the experience in shorthand and the same way each time: "the sight and smell of violets." This says, in effect, same stimulus same sensation. And this throttles adequate description and pinches off what is distinctly human and distinctly voluminous and centering in our lives.

What is actually perceived, just as it is perceived? Following Husserl, Gurwitsch calls this "the perceptual noema." Gurwitsch couples his analysis and description of this with fundamental work in Gestalt psychology— the study of autochthonous, apparently self-organizing perceived wholes. With these he opens the field famously entered and exploited by Maurice Merleau-Ponty in *The Phenomenology of Perception*. (New York: The Humanities Press, 1962. Merleau-Ponty is strangely reticent to acknowledge Gurwitsch's influence.[18]) By exploding the fictitious unit "stimulus-sensation," the whole world as immediately experienced is opened for fresh description. Opened are the involvements we bodily beings live immediately. Opened are the horizons of world-experienced and experienceable—awesome and exciting horizons. Phenomenology is pregnant with ontology, most emphatically with the restoration of the meaning and reality of self.

Aron Gurwitsch wrote across a broad spectrum of subject matters, from philosophy of mathematics, to philosophy of logic and of science, to phenomenology in its many incarnations. (Some of his writing has not been translated, and some of it has not been published at all.) But for the purposes of this essay, I must focus and limit my treatment of this important thinker.

William Barrett is generally credited with introducing existentialism to the United States in his 1947 *Partisan Review* article, "What is Existentialism?"[19] He had served in Europe in World War II and was alive to what seemed new possibilities of thought and living. He had long studied William James, and he thought of him as an existentialist before the term was invented.[20] He was also a greatly learned student of the history of philosophy, particularly with respect to Aristotle and medieval figures; and he liked to trace existential strands throughout our history's length.

Barrett's first job after his Ph.D. (from Columbia with work on Aristotle's *Physics*) was as assistant professor of mathematics in Chicago. We have seen how mathematics plays some key role in major phenomenologists from Peirce through Husserl to Gurwitsch. Barrett never lost his love of mathematics and would carry on lively discussions with the mathematicians at New York University where he taught for many years. He would often speak of the "soft underbelly of analytic philosophy," the inability of many analysts to understand the philosophical issues and opportunities in the philosophy of mathematics.

But each phenomenologist we have just mentioned adopts a somewhat different attitude toward math. I never heard Barrett speak of Peirce, and that genius is seldom mentioned in his writings. Barrett was particularly concerned with the tendency of mathematics on the level of arithmetic to hypostatize numbers and to project fictitious unities or units into our description of the immediately experienced world. (Of course, Peirce was way beyond that; but still. . . .)

Thus Barrett was very critical of Husserl's notion of intentional objects of thought as *noemata* (singular, *noema*). Despite all of Husserl's sophistication, Barrett believed, he retains a residuum of Cartesian subjectivism, intellectualism, and the mathematical hypostatizing found in "a sense datum" or the fictitious unit, "stimulus-sensation." We are left divided from Nature by a kind of veil, a broader, more elaborate, more luxurious veil to be sure, but still a veil. (I regret that I never asked Barrett and Harmon Chapman if they had influenced each other in this matter. I suspect that they had. See note 13.)

Even in the more sophisticated work of Gurwitsch on noemata, we are still not as open as we should be to immediate engagements, contingencies, involvements, engulfments in the experienced world fading out in the margins of awareness, so Barrett thought. Gurwitsch had elaborated an ontology of "objects," grouped in their regional domains. (Recall James's work in *Principles,* in "The Perception of Reality," on "the many worlds," with the perceived "world of practical realities" in space and time as the base-line for ordering all the other worlds—mythic, mathematical, fictional, insane, etc.) Each regional group of "objects" hangs together as a group according to its own principles of relevance or coherence. Groups hang together and are ordered in terms of ontological relevance or coherence. Principles of relevance and coherence are discovered by a phenomenologically ordered transcendental investigation of a flexible kind.

This is all very interesting, Barrett thinks, and he is aware that Gurwitsch is aware that discarding the "constancy hypothesis" opens up an area for de facto or incipient "phenomenological reduction," or unpacking of meaning. But still there is the noema. The perceptual noema in this case, but still the noema. There is an imported, a factitious, unit here, an encasing that impedes the free unfolding of our being in the world, in all its vagueness, perplexities, occludedness, unboundedness, its tantalizing horizons.

Barrett regards the arts as de facto phenomenological reductions and free variations on our situatedness in the world. The arts are as essential as is philosophy for revealing the many aspects and wrinkles of basal meaning. (But I can almost hear him say, Bruce, you phrase it in too Husserlian a way!) The arts must be complemented by the conceptual rigor of philosophy; but they complement philosophy in turn, for they are not as apt as discursive prose to be tripped into hypostatized concepts, abstractions, factitious units and unities.[21]

Barrett matrixed all his insights and descriptions in his study of history, intellectual and otherwise. He liked to quote Hegel, as I did earlier: *Wesen ist was ist gewesen.* Being is what has become. He was practically obsessed with tracing modern history from Descartes to the present. How did we wind up so powerful in certain respects, and so bewildered and impotent in others? Technology has engaged us momentously in the world, beyond our abilities to imagine the consequences of what we have done and are doing, and yet we are distanced and alienated, lonely and dispirited, many of us. Just how did it happen? Surely it has something to do with the Cartesian assumptions of the isolated ego-self, "the thing that thinks." Not even Kant's tremendous, watershed efforts are sufficient to reengage us with the world, heart and soul. Even Heidegger is skeletal at key points, and flesh and blood must be supplied by ourselves, so Barrett maintained.

In what is perhaps Barrett's masterwork, *The Illusion of Technique,* (Garden City, New York: Doubleday-Anchor, 1978), he argues at length that technology cannot assess its own assumptions, the ones that drive and limit it. It is philosophical work that must be done by thinkers who are phenomenological in the most supple, creative, and shrewd ways. His last work is the slim *Death of the Soul: From Descartes to the Computer* (Garden City, New York: Doubleday-Anchor, 1986). He traces the same path with some new ruminations. How did we possibly get *here!*? What can we do about it now? Will analytic philosophers ever wake up to the technologized reality in which we are embedded today, and to the philosophical challenges this fact thrusts in our faces? How long can Cartesian mock-battles go on? (One day he said under his breath, "Maybe boredom will finally get to them." At a distance now of 40 years, I think he may have suffered a moment's over-optimism.)

As I noted earlier, American phenomenology tends to be more balanced than its European counterparts often are. Essential to this balance, I think, are that Americans, on the whole, have their feet more broadly planted and braced within the history of philosophy (I ignore Heidegger, for the moment).

Let us proceed to our last figure, Calvin Schrag. His work is also broadly historically situated, though more systematic perhaps in its development of themes than is the case with Wild's and Barrett's work.

As I write, only Calvin Schrag still lives, of the phenomenologists discussed. He has spent nearly his whole career at Purdue University in Indiana. From his first book, decades ago, *Existence and Freedom* (Evanston: Northwestern University Press, 1961) until what I take to be his most recent, *The Self After Post-Modernity* (1997), Schrag exemplifies the basic insight that phenomenological description must precede scientific explanation. When this principle is ignored, we get premature and misleading explanation. The diversion typically takes this form: the coherence of the directly lived world is missed. The world is parcelled out, partialed out, into reified abstractions. The most obvious cut isolates self, mind, ego, subjectivity, on the one hand, over against the material or "external" world on the other. Phony problems are generated: How can "non extended" mind possibly influence "extended body," mine or any other's? How can minding self know there is anything beyond whatever is given in subjectivity—one's own privacy? Is there a world out there at all? How can value judgments possibly be true of ourselves and the rest of the world rather than being mere expressions of each of our subjective and idiosyncratic feelings and opinions? How can nihilism and vaporization of self be fended off?

Schrag's phenomenology restores the integrity of the world-immediately-experienced and undercuts and collapses artificial polar oppositions and dichotomies. It explodes, as well, attendant reifications of abstractions. The history of substantialism in all its forms is overhauled. Schrag criticises particularly the notion of the autonomous self as the seat of pure reason, or as that which looks on while the phenomenal world is constituted out of eternal Ideas, or by an Absolute Mind. The corollary of this alleged constitution is that the physical or extended world is regarded as the mere instantiation of eternal Ideas (or in modern physics as instances of laws, perhaps statistical only). The phenomenal presence of the physical world in all its amplitude, contingency, resistance, intimacy, and fluency is cut into fragments and frozen, including one's own body, one's body-self.

These premodern substantialist notions are discarded by Schrag, particularly the view of self (and Self and Mind) as center and ground of all reality and all knowledge. But also postmodern critiques of modernism are severely criticized by Schrag. He believes that the postmodernists have not husbanded the integrity of the world-phenomenon, but have themselves fallen into mindless dichotomies that, ironically, are left over from modernism: reason/irreason, universal/particular, self/nonself. As if the previously hidden member of siamese twins were to be shockingly turned to the fore by the postmodernists. From supposedly all-unifying pure reason they flip to the utter fragmentation of reason. From self they flip to the fear—or is it bravado—that there is no self, no powers of unification or direction at all.

Schrag gladly grants that the premodern idea of the substantial self must be discarded. But the postmodern notion of no-self (or something perilously close to that) does not follow. He plots a third way: his idea of a decentered self—all the while realizing that the notion of centeredness, and its companion decenteredness, is a crude spatial idea applicable only to an "external world" and its polarized and frozen companion, the "internal" domain.[22] Schrag quotes William James in *Essays in Radical Empiricism,* "The world experienced (otherwise called 'the field of consciousness') comes at all times with our body as its centre, centre of vision, centre of action, centre of interest." But on James's own idea of pre-reflective consciousness ("sciousness"—and Schrag agrees), body is not given at the center of the field of the world experienced, but as the ever warm and abiding animating presence on the margins of the field. Though marginal, it can be made focal when occasion calls for this (when the body is injured, say). But as marginal—and it is never wholly nonmarginal—it is the taproot of acts of abstraction, reasoning, and goal directedness, when that is appropriate.

Connected most intimately with the concept of decentered self is that of transversal rationality.[23] Gone is the "autonomous rational subject" issuing dicta to the contingent world beneath it. Present is the idea of an earthbound and earth-navigating reasoning that cuts across petrified dichotomies, reifications, hierarchies. Schrag develops Sartre's appropriation of Husserl's early *The Phenomenology of Internal Time Consciousness.* Appropriated is the concept of intentionalities transversing the stream of consciousness: the immediate past experienced and the immediate future anticipated tie together the recollected and anticipated time of one's whole life. Schrag also appropriates Peirce's and James's notion of reason as navigational "seat of the pants" reasoning. It has evolved over millions of years because it has gotten us where we need to get often enough to satisfy basic needs and interests (see for example James's "The Sentiment of Rationality"—rationality as the flowing of feelingful, working, discovering awareness). Given our survival needs, experience is self-organizing if it perdures at all, which recalls Gurwitsch's emphasis on the autochthonous nature of experience. Found throughout Schrag's work are also key references to A. N. Whitehead and his brilliant ideas of continuity and creativity.

Transversal rationality is chastened rationality. It aims for convergence of viewpoints and interests, personal and cultural, instead of strict identity or isomorphism of them. It sorts the world into kinds, universals, but without routinized assumptions concerning the ontological status of universals. It is an achievement of body-selves intimately involved, more than likely mimetically engulfed, in the rest of the world. Rationality is an achievement of us selves that are over our heads in the world.

As an achievement, our rational capacities are also subject to failure at any time. For example, Schrag quotes Felix Guattari on transversal rationality in groups.[24] How do the various staff members of a hospital, say, in their different roles and immediate interests, coordinate their activities to promote the welfare of the whole? It is a difficult task easily subject to failure.

Moreover, since selves are not born autonomous, they can only hope for, and work for, existential or moral autonomy. And since the individual's identity is all tied up with the identity of the group, any threat to the identity of the group may translate into frenzied purging of anything perceived to be alien—genocide. Schrag's work opens this gruesome topic for further inquiry.[25]

This philosopher's thought over his lifetime so far exhibits a marvelous consummatory sweep and balance. He recognizes that reason must be chastened, but to throw it away is mad. Likewise we must confront our finitude, vulnerability, contingency as bodily and social selves; but to simply discard belief in self—or to try to—is mad. We must recognize that our world has in fact fragmented into different spheres, the technological, the political-economic, the private, the institutional-religious. But to simply throw up our hands and despair over this massive malcoordination is senseless. We must work together to find our way through the world. Without a measure of success in doing this, we ineluctably social and communicative beings come unhinged.

The ultimate challenge to transversal rationality is to achieve transversal transcendence. That is, not an idling on top of an imagined pyramid, not an attempted domination of the spheres of human activity, but a connecting and chastened ordering of them insofar as they are knowable and changeable by us. We must achieve a rationality that navigates and orients itself through these spheres of activity in some tolerable way.

Not to be swallowed up in one or other of these spheres requires the recognition that none of them is our ultimate concern, only preliminary and contingent. Our ultimate concern is with the ground of Being, that within which we emerge stage by stage, and that which sustains us every minute. Our ultimate concern is to be overfull, to pour ourselves out in unconditional respect and love, and to be prepared to receive it. We will live stunted if we cannot transcend contractual relationships. Even subtle ones in which friendship is between equals who can expect to get, more or less, as good as they give. We learn with little surprise that as a graduate student at Harvard years ago, Schrag was Paul Tillich's assistant—Tillich, the author of *The Courage to Be.*

One of Calvin Schrag's keenest insights into postmodernist thinkers is that some in this brightly bannered camp (e.g., J-F Lyotard) have muddled together the ahistorical and the transhistorical. In throwing out the former, they tend to throw out the latter. But to do that is to miss the abidingly human, our primal needs and skills developed in the course of evolution. Our primal need for symbolical meaning distinguishes us from the other creatures, but does not separate us—not if we are wise. In this, Schrag reminds us of John Wild, and indeed of so many phenomenologists in the United States who, as I said, exhibit a balance and historical depth that distinguishes them from some of their flashier Continental counterparts.

Notes

1. Husserl might be thought to hold to brute thats: he gives the example of picking up a drinking glass absentmindedly. Expecting it to be water, say, it is milk. Our expectation exploded in the instant, we don't know *what* it is. It is mere sensuous matter, a brute that. No wonder we have the urge to spit it out! James and Peirce might agree. But none of them believe that we have discovered pure Being, out of which evolves dialectically the universe. James's idea of "*thats* that are ready to become all kinds of *whats*" is integral to his idea of "pure experience," and this is basic in all of his *Essays in Radical Empiricism.*

2. Kenneth L. Ketner, *His Glassy Essence: An Autobiography of Charles Sanders Peirce* (Nashville: Vanderbilt University Press, 1998), p. 296. A new departure in Peirce studies.

3. Same, p. 306.

4. See my *William James and Phenomenology: A Study of "The Principles of Psychology"* (Bloomington and London: Indiana University Press, 1968 [New York: AMS Press, 1979]).

5. William James, "The Experience of Activity," in his *Essays in Radical Empiricism* (New York: Longmans, Green, and Co., 1912), pp. 160 ff. Included in part in my anthology, *The Essential Writings of William James,* pp. 206 ff.

6. William James, *The Principles of Psychology,* vol. 1 (New York: Dover Books, 1950 [1890]), p. 231. Also in my anthology, p. 148.

7. See again my *William James and Phenomenology,* pp. 4, 120.

8. The same, p. 120. For Horizon, James is obviously indebted to R. W. Emerson. As a boy, James heard that redoubtable and irrepressible man discourse at length in the James home.

9. Edmund Husserl, *Cartesian Meditations,* trans. by Dorion Cairns (The Hague: M. Nijhoff, 1965), p. 100.

10. Brice Wachterhauser, *Phenomenology and Skepticism: Essays in Honor of James Edie,* Introduction (Evanston, IL: Northwestern University Press, 1996), p. 12.

11. I have already cited these writings, but since they are so important, and since many analytic philosophers are ignorant of their existence, I cite them again. Bernard Baars, *In the Theatre of Consciousness: The Workspace of the Mind.* Bruce Mangan, "Taking Phenomenology Seriously: The 'Fringe' and its Implications for Cognitive Research," in *Consciousness and Cognition* 2, pp. 89–108.

12. See my "Passion for Meaning: William Ernest Hocking's Religious-Philosophical Views," *Transactions of the C. S. Peirce Society* 33, no. 4 (fall, 1997). Also in my *The Primal Roots of American Philosophy: Pragmatism, Phenomenology, and Native American Thought* (University Park: Penn State University Press, 2000).

13. See Wild's anthology and manifesto for this group: John Wild, *Return to Reason, Essays in Realistic Philosophy* (Chicago: The University Press, 1953). Note particularly Harmon Chapman's fine contribution in which he argues for a realistic construal of phenomenological themes, e.g., intentionality. For Chapman, Husserl mistakenly thought that the intentional relationship of thinking to thought-about was "capped at both ends," when it should be closed only at the end of the finite ego-thinker. That is, the thought-about as world is to be grasped as presenting itself with open horizons. Also note Chapman's acute critique of Husserl's notion of *hyletic* mental data as an uncritical residuum of Cartesian and British empiricist mentalism, sense-data-ism: *Sensations and Phenomenology* (Bloomington: Indiana University Press, 1967).

14. See Wild's *Plato's Modern Enemies, and the Theory of Natural Law* (Chicago: The University Press, 1953), pp. 10, 69, 109, 230 ff.

15. Aron Gurwitsch, *The Field of Consciousness* (Pittsburg: Duquesne University Press, 1964 [trans.]), p. 70.

16. Note James Edie's excellent "Phenomenology in the United States," *Journal of the British Society for Phenomenology* 5, no. 3 (October 1974), pp. 204–211.

17. William James, *The Principles of Psychology,* vol I, pp. 194–195.

18. James Edie, "Phenomenology in the United States," p. 207.

19. See Wiliam Barrett, *What is Existentialism?* (New York: Free Press, 1964).

20. "Of all the non-European philosophers, William James probably best deserves to be labelled an Existentialist. Indeed . . . we may very well wonder if it would not be more accurate to call James an Existentialist than a Pragmatist." William Barrett, *Irrational Man* (New York: Doubleday-Anchor, 1962 [1958]) p. 18.

21. Barrett thus criticized my dissertation, later published as *William James and Phenomenology:* (Bloomington: Indiana University Press, 1968) "Too much Husserl." But he was pleased when I published, *Role Playing and Identity: The Limits of Theatre as Metaphor* (Bloomington: Indiana University Press, 1991 [1982]), and also articles that treated theatre as de facto phenomenological "reductions" or free variations on human situatedness and action, a phenomenology of the act *in act, ambulando.* "Robert Wilson's Theatre as a De Facto Phenomenological Reduction," *Philosophy and Social Criticism* 5, no. 1, 1978. And "Theatre as Phenomenology: The Disclosure of Historical Life," *Annals of Scholarship,* Special issue, Summer 1982. For some of Barrett's own philosophical studies of art (with no positive mention of Husserl), see his study of Hemingway, for example, in *Irrational Man,* and all of *Time of Need: Forms of Imagination in the Twentieth Century* (New York: Harper & Row, 1972), particularly chapt. 4, "Backward Toward the Earth."

22. See Calvin Schrag, *Communicative Praxis and the Space of Subjectivity* (Bloomington: Indiana University Press, 1986), pp. 139 ff.

23. See first and foremost Calvin Schrag, *The Resources of Rationality: A Response to the Postmodern Challenge* (Bloomington: Indiana University Press, 1992), pp. 148 ff.

24. Calvin Schrag, *The Self After Postmodernity* (New Haven and London: Yale University Press, 1997), pp. 131–133.

25. See my essay in this volume, "Conceptual Problems in Grasping Genocide." Also my "Decentered Subjectivity, Transversal Rationality, and Genocide" in a Festschrift for Schrag, Northwestern University Press, 2001. The first of these is a compression of a book-length manuscript—*Making the World Pure for God: Genocide, Terrorism, and Human Nature*—and the second is a preliminary study for it.

5
Nature or Nurture?:
The Significance of Indigenous Thought

The earth and myself are of one mind. The measure of the land
and the measure of our bodies are the same.

—Joseph, Chief, Nez Perce

With regard to some bit of behavior, somebody asks, Is it due to nature or nurture? Now, why are we so sure that it must be either nature or nurture, and not, say, both? Or why not more than two something or others? Why not twenty-two?

Surely our parents belong on the nurture side of the alleged opposed pair, nature/nurture? But they're mammalian organisms, aren't they, the products of millions of years of evolution in nature? The baby cries, the nursing mother lactates. The very question, Is that nature or nurture?— one and not the other?—limits and distorts the inquiry into what's happening.

Ah, but surely the genes we inherit are pure nature? Not so quick. Geneticists tell us that the genes themselves evolved over millions of years in at least minimally nurturing environments. Moreover, and this is a huge point, which genes "turn on" today, manifest themselves, is in part a function of what the current environment nurtures rather than discourages and suppresses.

If we ask, say, What is Nature in itself? Right off the bat, we have prejudiced the inquiry. For this "in itself" must generate its counter "in itself," something that's supposed to do the nurturing: "nurturing in itself." "Nature in itself" generates its grotesque Siamese twin, "nurturing in itself." Or, "Nature in itself" generates its twin, "humanity in itself."

And this abortive development hatches, in turn, a disastrous binary opposition between ecologies: "nature based ecologies" opposed to "human based ones." The possibility of any inclusive, coherent ecology—any single view of our relationships as actual whole body-selves in the actual whole world—is nipped in the bud. How we human organisms might best contribute to the value of Nature becomes a question that loses its grip. And, on the other hand, how our "spirituality" (and mentality) is integral to the whole world: that investigation wanders off into pathetically misguided New Age attempts to rise above the "darkness of the body," and so forth. To rise above our own kinesthesis and motility, our own marvelous interior processes, cavities, muscular and neural adaptations attuned over millions of years to the world around us! What could more mislead?

Chief Joseph is right: "the earth and our bodies are of one mind." Because "the measure of the land and the measure of our bodies are the same." That is, mind, or our minding, is done by our minding body. And our minding or "measuring" bodies cannot be divorced from the world minded or measured. This is what we are! We are minding or measuring bodies, and most basically so in the actual sensuous presence of the actual world all around us. Mind, spirit, nurture, culture is not a domain independent of Nature.

I conversed recently with an academic-analytic philosopher who fancies himself an environmental ethicist or ecologist. He suggested a cure for overuse of the Grand Canyon. Build a virtual reality theatre for tourists near the canyon, and keep them out of the canyon entirely. When I said that this sounded like a council of despair, he looked at me uncomprehendingly. He would never know what the visitors, under his plan, would never know: full bodily and mental-spiritual involvement in the real Canyon.

Let's try to stop this crude and abusive slicing of reality into Nature and nurture, or Nature and human, or matter and mind. Nothing exists only in itself: everything is related in some way to everything else. Nevertheless, to think simplistically of "Nature in itself" is for us nurtured, civilized beings to think Nature, or experience it, however glancingly and misleadingly. How can we refer to anything in any way meaningfully unless we assume that it is experienceable in some way and to some extent by us? Even if we imagine reaches of Nature in space-time not to be actually experienceable by us, it is still our imagining, our experiencing in the mode of imagining. And in so imagining we do get something meaningful to us: the ultimately mysterious. The Plains Indians named this

Wakan Tanka, and other tribes used cognate locutions. They are best translated as the Great Mystery.

A lot of well-intentioned ecological thinking must be abandoned: all that simplistically opposes Nature's interests to humans' interests. For a precondition of all civilizing and nurturing of humans is that we exist as organisms in Nature, as organisms formed in Nature over millions of years of prehuman and human adaptation. Civilizations, then, are modifications of Nature wrought by human organisms, but always—and this is dreadfully easy to forget—always within Nature.

So, as John Dewey knew long ago, the super-objective of all true education is to foster continuity: the development of the natural and spontaneous into the artful and cultivated. The development of spontaneous smiling into the artful smiling in which we greet guests at a formal dinner, for instance. The spontaneous and natural should be the abiding matrix of our lives. (But there's no such thing as a natural smile? Put plates of good food before very hungry people and see what happens to their faces.)

The problem is not the evolution of human culture and enculturation *per se* (whatever that means exactly!), for the inexpugnable fact is that enculturation of human organisms will always occur within Nature, like it or not. There *is* a terrible problem, and it is that this enculturation, spurred by science and technology, has proceeded eruptively rapidly. So rapidly that, again as John Dewey noted, new meanings or "measures" of things are jammed into our body-selves or body-minds half-baked. These clog and disrupt the natural fluency and continuity of good manners, that is, our full and harmonious functioning as organisms over millions of years of adaptations within Nature. These half-baked meanings disrupt the continuity of Nature and culture.

Nowhere are the disruptions of human functioning prompted by science and technology more disturbingly evident than in the genetic discoveries being made right now. We are human organisms modifying not only the genetic structures of the food we eat, animal and vegetable, but our own genetic structure. "Design your own brain"—such slogans are in the air.

But it *should* be obvious: to design ourselves *well*, we must use our current brains well; and genetic science and engineering by themselves cannot supply the criteria by which we could tell if we were designing ourselves well. Such criteria could only be derived from a study of what humankind over the many millennia of our development have found most fulfilling.

And it is just this prehistory and history that science and technology are rapidly covering over and losing. Science and technology raise such a multicolored cloud of dust that what's being done to our own lives is hidden.

To many of course it seems clear: So you want beautiful and smart kids? Then fertilize models' eggs with sperm from decent looking male M.D.'s and Ph.D.'s. This quasi-informed, actually naive prescription is appalling. "Well then," it might be said, "don't trust the combinatorial chances of traditional sexual reproduction: clone a single exemplar human being (which soon will be possible, I suppose). And, to forestall your charge of naivete, raise it in circumstances similar to those in which the exemplar was raised."

The naivete at this point is more than appalling, it is stupefying. Such champions of science and technology have become so dazzled in glittering abstractions and self-sealing conceptions that the reality of time itself—days, months, years, generations—is no longer felt. It *should* be obvious: a clone cannot be raised in a manner similar to the original, the exemplar, if for no reason other than he or she is a clone, and cannot have any *parents*. And besides, the whole world is one generation—a quasi-generation—different and older, other from, what it was. Geneticism is a form of scientism, a wandering and babbling in the fog of quasi-mystery.

Here is a fact of cosmical-human significance, if I can put it so: the only model we have of good, vital, creative, sustainable human life are the countless generations of heterosexually procreated human beings, from the Paleolithic down to now, life-nurtured and structured within time-tested cultures of humans-in-Nature over many millennia.

We have almost completely destroyed indigenous cultures, our models. We technology-driven modern humans have not been around long enough to prove we are viable. In only a few hundred years of modern science we have altered the globe and our own bodily rhythms, producing many forms of disequilibrium and discontinuity, for example, manifold addictions (see my *Wild Hunger: The Primal Roots of Modern Addiction*, Lanham, MD and New York: Rowman and Littlefield, 1998). And we have in our hands the atomic means to poison the planet for 10,000 years. Looming before us now is the possibility or probability of genetic pollution as well: the release of genes from one species that are pathogenic when lodged in another species. These pathogenic genes are immune to any known antidote.

We are far from proving we are a viable and sustainable version of homo sapiens. I soon return to these points.

Genetic scientists themselves are not quite as naive as their engineer-entrepreneur colleagues. Among their discoveries is, as I said, the fact that while some genes turn on nearly no matter what, others turn on only as a function of environment, as a function of the particular stimulation, support, or meaning that the particular environment affords.

Science must limit its vocabulary to generate its precise predictions and quantitative results. This limits its ability to *describe* environments so thoroughly that it might predict just which range of environments will turn on which genes, with which effects. For it is not only what observing, measuring, experimenting scientists say about the nature and power of environments that characterize these. But also what the beings who've developed over generations within these environments say and feel and believe about them. It is a matter of the mythic systems of belief, tacit or manifest, through which they experience environments.

What does a particular environment *mean* to a people caught up immediately and traditionally within it? Caught up within its traditional mytho-poeic framework of interpretation and guidance. And, again, it is just this whole lengthily evolved prescientific background and framework that the dust and racket of contemporary scientific and technological breakthroughs destroys or obscures.

Far from answering philosophical questions about who we are and what is best for us, marvelous discoveries in genetics, for example, only expand, deepen, and darken the questions.

Let me elaborate a bit. To try to formulate genetic laws, geneticists know they must specify a standard environment. But this raises a huge—I think a staggering—question. What is the standard environment for human organisms evolved over millions of years in Nature? That is, what is the environment in which we have survived and taken shape and often flourished over all this time? It was an environment of hunting and gathering in which we big-brained, bipedal, dexterously handed organisms took shape by adapting through time-proven skills, virtues, rituals, and beliefs. Our forebears were hunter-gatherers.

Geneticists must specify standard environments in terms that fit their experimental practices and theories, for example standard cultures in standard Petri dishes, or standard crystals for standard microscopes. They must side-step the meaning of standard environment for whole selves in whole environments. But it is these wholes that establish the lived meaning and value of what humans experience in environments. To simply assume that this holistic meaning is irrelevant to which genes turn off and on? That must be proved. If it is not, we must charge scientists with dogmatism.

For 99 percent of the time of genus homo's presence on earth, we were hunter-gatherers! The radical shift into a more sedentary agricultural way of life occurred a mere 10,000 years ago, spearheaded by land-hungry, highly aggressive, agricultural states. After tumultuous wars, agricultural life passed relatively quickly into industrial, which passed much more rapidly into atomic and electronic. This is now accelerating and moving us at a dizzying rate, generating consequences beyond our best abilities to calculate or even imagine.

So how could we possibly grasp the meaning of what we're doing as we go about "managing" things? It may be only a short time before desperately bored—or just desperate—people employ horrific powers to tie up or destroy our electronically, genetically, and ballistically interconnected world. Again, it is not clear that we modern technologized humans will survive. There has not yet elapsed enough time to test.

Like it or not, those ancient hunter-gatherers, existing, thinking, and dreaming in wilderness for hundreds of thousands of years, are the best model we have of vital, sustainable human life. During all this time our species adapted and took shape. This was the standard environment. In our time of so-called progress we have nearly exterminated our best models—their kinship with Earth, the plants, the other animals, the birds—these primal persons' profound symbolisms, excitements, contentments gone.

The aim of all education is today systematically missed; and this is the development in continuity of encultured and artful ways out of natural, instinctive, spontaneous ones (though there is nothing infallible about these latter).

Some geneticists speak of some environments as hijacking genes. If this is so, we can only wonder what the precipitous breakup of traditional human groups, human skills, sacred beliefs, rites of passage are doing to our total genetic welfare. As TV, video, and Internet connect us, and at the same time jumble the experienced world as a whole into bright disconnected bits, what is happening to us? As faceless international capital dictates the fate of the world's peoples, what is happening to our feel for people face to face, our sense of intimate cooperation and primitive equity, our sense of personal and social responsibility? What is happening to our gut sense of our reality and identity as individuals with the responsibility and dignity to choose the right thing, whether at any one moment we feel like doing it or not?

At the time of the so-called triumph of the West, why do so many people feel so crappy, so lonely, so abandoned? Why so much dysthymia (a scientistic coinage meaning simple unhappiness)? There is increased longevity, but what's the point if it means more time for boredom, for vague immune dysfunctions like allergies, and for the horrendous plague of addictions that settles upon us, from workaholism to the grimmest heroin afflictions?

How on earth do we find the standard environment today, that baseline which will allow geneticists to determine the full range of genetic laws for the turning on or off of genes? There is no hope whatsoever without grasping the full force and reach of "environment" as that has formed our species over myriad years. I quote again how David Abram returns us in thought to our nearly forgotten home, our hunting-gathering forebears:

> Our bodies have formed themselves in delicate reciprocity with the manifold textures, sounds, and shapes of an animate earth—our eyes have evolved in subtle interaction with other eyes, as our ears are attuned by their very structure to the howling of wolves and honking of geese.

But Abram goes on,

> I found myself now observing the heron from outside its world, noting with interest its careful, high-stepping walk and the sudden dart of its beak into the water, but no longer feeling its tensed yet poised alertness with my own muscles.

When such alienation and objectification is endemic in a culture, there is vast trouble.

We, our very selves in our immediacy, commune with and incorporate these very animals. Other creatures' seeings and soundings and movings are built into our bodies, are woven through our musculature, our nervous systems, very probably over millions of years of adaptation into our genes. A funded community of intercorporeality exists as a vibrant residuum in our body-selves, a legacy from paleolithic times. The residuum is now greatly disturbed.

Genetic engineers can easily pinch down their awareness to encompass only immediate palpable gains, such as those gained by manipulating the genetic code of corn to render it immune to a list of diseases. Caught in tunnel vision, possibilities of long-term and far-ranging destructive effects are masked out, and the masking is masked out. Occluded are intricate balances and delicate interrelationships worked out over millions of years of evolution that constitute the very identities of things. Monarch butterflies seem to suffer from feeding on the pollen of genetically engineered corn. What might be the deleterious long-term effects on human organisms, thousands of times more massive? (See Mae Won Ho, *Genetic Engineering: Dream or Nightmare?* New York: Continuum Publishing Co., 2000 [1998]) Caught within the means-ends tunnel vision of technological thinking, we need to be jolted out of it. Then we need to take a deep breath and to look around.

It's become a cliche: scientists and technicians are playing God. Too bad for an immense truth to be dulled this way! For, to use one of Loren Eisley's phrases, we live within "the firmament of time," the nearly unimaginable depth of time. We "bright ones" tend to think that we can improve on the community of intercorporeality built up over countless millennia. It is a community in which human and nonhuman, animal and vegetable identities were constituted through intertwining or interfusing with each other *and* being distinguished from each other. So we presume to now mix human and nonhuman genes to produce an optimal animal for certain tasks, one that can work like a horse and do minimal calculations, say.

But *what* have we produced? We don't know! Does it have rights? We don't know! Is it a perfect slave? We don't know! Completely out of touch with the trial-and-error wisdom of the vast depth of time, with the slowly and intricately worked out adaptations of things, we don't know what we've done. We babble stupefied in quasi, man-made mystery—which means muddle. To think that science and technology can answer all the questions that their own brilliance and competence have generated, is to confuse being out to lunch with remaining at work.

In the genetic revolution we find new evidence for Nietzsche's, and others', belief that we modern Europeans and Euro-Americans lack depth.

Nature or nurture? If ever there were a vexingly conceptual and philosophical issue, this is it. But there are deeply rooted dualistic and oppositional prejudices in much of the most disciplined and, one might think, reliable philosophical thinking. The urge to separate mind or minding from "mere" matter is one that most thinkers find it impossible to resist. This is somewhat understandable. For mind or minding is always *of* or *about* something. Whereas mere matter seems to be just objects "in themselves," knocking into each other or influencing each other in some way, no doubt. But these objects are not *of* or *about* something in the way that a thought is of what is thought about. There seems to be something distinctively mental in individual or group mind or minding.

There are genuine philosophical and conceptual difficulties here. For my purposes in this essay, I limit myself to the following. Since the seventeenth century, the natural sciences have proved sensationally successful. So successful have they been that many trained thinkers believe that eventually everything will be explained by them (insofar as anything is ever explained). The natural sciences adopt what some, such as Thomas Nagel, have called "the view from nowhere." That is, scientists worldwide should be able to agree if they investigate long enough, no matter how different their local cultural or personal viewpoints might be. Natural science is mathematical science, and mathematics and scientific measurements are universal.

So it is at least understandable that thinkers should believe that local cultural and personal viewpoints are "merely subjective," are of subordinate importance. For they believe that all explanation must be in terms of natural science, the view from nowhere. The merely subjective and mental, "views from somewhere" will ultimately be explained—if explained at all—in terms of the view from nowhere, so they believe.

Now almost inevitably this faith in science creates difficulties for understanding the roles of Nature and nurture. Almost inevitably we get constriction of view and reductionism. The investigation of what environments in all their manifold layers and levels *mean* to people traditionally and immediately attuned to them tends to be short-changed. But without understanding this we cannot understand what environments fully *are.* And without understanding that, we get no definitive account of which genes turn off or on as a function of environment.

The belief in the omnicompetence of natural science goes like this: "The only hope for really explaining things lies in the view from nowhere, natural science." For my part, until I see proof otherwise, I believe this faith in science to be an example of scientism, not science. That is, the belief that only science, as we know it, can know, and that other claims to know are mere subjective opinion.

I reiterate: scientism cannot be supported by science itself. For to substantiate the claim that other ways of knowing are fraudulent, or unreliable, would require that science pursue these putative ways of knowing and determine that they get us nowhere. But to pursue these other ways systematically and reliably would either require science to abandon its own proven methods and scope of validity; or, to rule a priori and arbitrarily that the other ways cannot possibly be effective in their subject-matter areas. Either way, science oversteps itself. Scientism is ideology, not science.

Even when science *explains,* we must first have an adequate *description* of the local viewpoints and sensuous and/or ritualistic experiencing that is to be explained. Adequate for what? Adequate for understanding just what is to be explained. That is, adequate for grasping the immediately lived meaning of our own lives, our views from somewhere as body-selves or body-minds (recall Chief Joseph).

When for any reason our actual, lived experiencing is slighted—say, our experiencing of intercorporeality and kinship with other species of animals—we tend to wither and to grow vacuous and desiccated. We don't need science to discover this for us (though science may discover some important things about why this is so). All we need are good observational and descriptive skills, and some empathic ones as well. I mean, we need to be in touch with ourselves and the land.

When the immediately lived, observed, and described meaning of our lives is regarded as a mere epiphenomenon of underlying causes to be discovered only by science, the importance of this meaning is discounted. With this we discount ourselves, and lose an important ingredient in understanding the relationship of Nature and nurture. I find it hard to believe that we can grasp how environments turn genes on or off without grasping how the world's felt presence moves us immediately, totally, re-generatively in manifold situations. Don't we need all the help we can get? From every angle? From our immediate, felt, local, first-person points of view and reactions mediated by mythic systems, as well as from "the view from nowhere," the scientific view?

We exist now in a time of most perilous disruption of the continuity of Nature and culture—also the disruption of the continuity of science and our own experiencing. Science and technology alone cannot save us.

Indeed, I believe that science and technology *alone* (insofar as anything can be alone) exacerbate disruption and discontinuity of Nature and culture, and increase the meaninglessness of life for the whole self in a whole environment. No mere cleverness and scientism can extract us, no mere fashioning of facile dualisms and oppositions can save us, nor can any amount of hypersimplified political rhetoric.

6

Conceptual Problems in Grasping Genocide

The earth hath bubbles as the water hath.

—Macbeth

Genocide seems to defy all reason. But we must assume there are reasons for it if we are to think about it at all.

Genocide might be construed as a form of warfare. But it must be sharply distinguished from war in the usual sense. The goal of conventional war is achieved when an enemy group's armed forces are defeated. But the point of genocide is to destroy *all* members of an alien group—men, women, children—even fetuses have sometimes been dug out of newly dead pregnant women and destroyed.

Now why? Why? There is something about that alien form of life that the home group, the genocidal group, finds absolutely intolerable, absolutely disgusting and unassimilable. Just what is it about that alien life?

There are horrifying and disgusting aspects of all warfare. But in conventional war there are typically moments of glory that drive and sustain some of the combatants through the horrors. The glory is typically missing in genocide. Norbert Elias, a student of violence in the middle ages, quotes from a knight's diary:

> War is a joyous thing. We love each other so much in war. . . . A sweet joy
> rises in our hearts, in the feeling of our honest loyalty to each other; and
> seeing our friend so bravely exposing his body to danger . . . This brings
> such delight that anyone who has not felt it cannot say how wonderful it is.
> Do you think that someone who feels this is afraid of death? Not in the
> least![1]

There is little delight or glory in genocide. More like a sense of duty prevails. Little bravery is involved. Typically innocent and helpless men, women, children are penned up and slaughtered. The Nazis (far from being the only genocidal group in the twentieth century but providing a vivid example) regarded extermination of those *others* as a distasteful duty that not every loyal member of the armed forces was up to. And those who were, were entitled to special periods of rest and recuperation.

Then, aren't genociders simply sadists, sociopaths and psychopaths, those without conscience who derive pleasure from others' pain? Doubtless such people are caught up in genocidal movements. But there simply aren't enough of them to do the work of genocide. Many "ordinary people" are caught up in it.

But then, one might say, there are *many* reasons or motivations for genocide. They must span the gamut of economic, sociological, biological, historical factors. Why should we expect a philosopher to supply much illumination?

I grant there are many factors involved, and that a philosopher can't be expected to span them all. But I suspect there's a key factor that is typically overlooked in the many accounts and explanations of genocide given over the years. And I think that this factor bristles with vexing conceptual issues of inherently philosophical moment and difficulty.

Our conventional categories of explanation—economic, sociological, biological, historical—do apply to genocide to some extent. But either singly or together they leave open big questions. Why do genociders try to eliminate all those others? Doddering old men and women, infants, even sometimes fetuses. Why, according to conventional categories, could these be felt to be a terrible threat to the state? The Nazis claimed that Jews were an economic threat, they claimed that Jewish bankers after World War I prompted inflation and snatched food from the mouths of good Germans.

But the Nazis also slaughtered the Gypsies, a million and a half of them. Nobody could cite the gypsies as an economic threat to the state, or any kind of conventional threat. Pol Pot emptied out the capitol city of Cambodia, Phom Penh, of its million plus inhabitants. He marched them into the forests and jungles where they couldn't survive, and/or he and his men clubbed them to death. They were classed as degenerate intellectuals and urbanites. But how could Cambodia be expected to survive and compete in the contemporary industrialized and electronified world without such people? (Pol Pot had spent years in France; what could he have been thinking?) Serbs and Muslims had lived for generations side by side in Bosnia, working together, intermarrying. But once Serb authorities influenced by Slobodon Milosovic branded the Muslims as *other*, practically overnight they became the targets of a hideous genocide. In the late nineteenth and early twentieth centuries, "Digger Indians" hiding out in the upper canyons of central California were used as target practice by Whites. How did they pose any kind of threat, as judged by conventional categories?

Genocide seems to defy all reason, at least in the conventional senses of reason! It is a philosopher's typically thankless job to try to expand what we can mean by "reason." Thankless, because people must try to understand with the reason they bring with them, that is, with the received, the conventional categories of understanding.

Genocide seems to defy all reason—to be irrational. But we must suppose there is *some* reason, or we who try to understand should pack up our tools and go home. Either that, or we must press on all imaginable notions of reason so hard that we can know there is no reason discoverable. But, how could we *know* that we have pressed as hard as possible on *all* imaginable notions of reason?

I think that I have some idea of the *X* factor in the explanation of genocide. It lies deeper than all conventional categories of explanation. All these categories presuppose this factor, albeit unwittingly. They all presuppose *the world* in which the events they purport to explain occur. Now how do any of us form the gut notion or meaning—vague but utterly fundamental—of the world? That is the question that serious thinkers must address.[2]

First of all, what is the meaning, or what are the meanings, of meaning? The meaning of anything, I believe, is our sense of its presence in our experience, and of its consequences for our experience, and its possible presence and consequences. In other words, the meaning of anything is our sense of its experienceability. What if we are philosophically inclined, and we push experienceability to its margins, imaginability? And what if we should then push imaginability to what we take its limits to be? We would imagine that there are events not experienceable by us. (Not experienceable beyond imagining *that* such unspecifiable sorts of events occur.) Even here we would get a rarified but fundamental meaning: the mysterious.

Now, the *world* is not meaningful on the same level as are events merely *in the world*. The latter events, of whatever sort, presuppose the utterly fundamental sense of world in which they occur. As infants and then as toddlers growing up we simply absorb unwittingly, by osmosis as it were, the sense of world that the authorities all around us have themselves brought with them to every situation. That is, we absorb our culture, and its taken-for-granted background sense of world, undeliberately.

We do this by what I call mimetic engulfment: undeliberate imitation of others.[3] Inexorably, our culture structures our neural, muscular, and glandular systems, our reality as minding organisms. John Dewey is right: our minding is our adapting, our coping on a gut level with the world around us, and only the smallest fraction of this coping ever gets into our consciousness, let alone into the focus of that.

Sometimes, on the far margins of their consciousness, people may get a glimmering, tremulous, fleeting feeling of the mysteriousness and questionability of *world,* as habitually and, finally, instinctively experienced by them and their group. But the feeling is not speakable, not acknowledgeable, not thematizable; most likely it is terrifying.

Refuge is immediately found in a renewed feeling of certainty about the world. Though this certainty is naive, it is absolutely necessary for most of us most of the time. World is simply "this here world." *Our* world, of course, our world-experienced and experienceable, our world-interpreted. But why would one even point this out, or ask the question whether it's ours or not? There is manifestly one world, right? And what could it be but our world-experienced and experienceable in our experiencing?!

I think this is the best path to the hidden X factor for explaining the occurrence of genocide. A group, shaky for any reason, encounters an alien group that experiences the world in terms different from the home group's habitual ways of experiencing the world. Its world-experienced is different from the home group's. The home group's world-experienced and experienceable shudders and begins to give way beneath its members' feet. Because the meaning of *world* is presupposed by the meaning of everything *in the world,* everything shakes and begins to collapse. There is psychophysical earthquake. In terror, the only world they know, the only reality that is theirs to know, teeters and trembles. A solution presents itself: exterminate or radically immobilize or displace the alien others.

And why destroy or discomfit *all* of them? Because each and every one of them carries the actuality or potentiality of the subversive, disruptive, alien way of experiencing the world, of constituting a rival world-experienced. Furthermore, since it's a matter of a disruptive and alien mode of experiencing or minding the world, every memory of that other way must be expunged. For even a memory of an alien way of experiencing and minding the world might infect the thinking and feeling of those who remember.

Thus Nazis razed and ploughed over Jewish cemeteries; also they removed evidence of the gypsies having once existed. Thus Bosnian Serbs shelled and burned the Oriental and the National museums in Sarajevo, for these contained evidence of centuries of coexistence of Serbs and Muslims. Thus evidence of the genocides of Native American groups in California was suppressed from Euro-American consciousness for many generations. Thus the genocide of Tutsis by Hutus in Rwanda, Africa, was virtually ignored while it was happening.

And why the horrifying occurrence of digging out and killing fetuses in pregnant women? Because every *possibility* of that alien mode of being, minding, experiencing must be eliminated. We find a monstrous aversion to that alien mode of life: it is experienced as life-threatening life—meddlesome, polluting, infecting life. The Nazis spoke of "life unworthy of life."

As it might be feared that one germ, no matter how isolated and ineffectual it may seem to be, may spread in contagion and fell a vast organism, so every instance of that alien life must be crushed. Consonant with this mental stance, we saw among the genociders in Argentina a few years back the hysterical dread of an alien mode of life, the subversive mode. One genocider is reported to have said that the swollen breasts of pregnant women "invite the prod," the electric cattle prod. Is this just the giggling of a particular sadist-pervert? Maybe not.

We thinkers must pitch in. All the fundamental questions must be raised again, and all at once, as it were. For example, what is the being of possibility—a question only sporadically and scantily treated since Aristotle. And what is the *individuum,* any individual, of any sort? We must try to combat the excessive atomism and individualism—thoughtless analysis—rampant in Western philosophy in so many different forms for so long. For instance, what on earth is *the mind,* of which many professional philosophers speak so easily? Either "an individual mind," or "*the* human mind?" Mystified by these abstractions, our gut sense of our own lives, just as we live then moment by moment, tends to be forgotten. Our sense of *our organisms' actual acts of minding—our-mindings-along-with-others-in-environments* tends to be forgotten.

I believe that only when we realize how our traditional thinking has forcibly abstracted individuals out of their groups will we begin to grasp the hidden dynamics of genocidal mayhem. We have lifted persons out of their groups and pasted the hypostatized word "individual" upon them. We do not see how persons are caught up by their groups, very often possessed by them, and I mean to suggest demonic possession.

We must finally understand individual *groups:* that is, the *corporate* individual. Only then will we understand how the shaking or wilting of the group can so profoundly derange its individual members. A truly basic need of the human individual is to be accepted by the group as a member. And what that individual *is* is very much a matter of the roles within the corporate individual which are open to him or her. Maybe there are no possibilities but one. How powerless that individual in his or her very individuality must feel!

In trying to understand genocide we need all the help we can get. When we see how puny and ineffectual many of our literal terms are, we see that some help must come from metaphors. Note how Ernst Cassirer's use of metaphor in the second volume of *The Philosophy of Symbolic Forms,* "Mythic Consciousness," helps us grasp the "shape" and "levels" of the corporate body.[4] (It will help us grasp how Nazis, for example, could think that Jews were infecting the *Volkskörper,* the body of the folk.)

Cassirer unpacks brilliantly the metaphor of the corporate body. He distinguishes these levels: the head, or chief setter of policy; the arms, the executives who carry out the head's orders and plans; the trunk and support staff who support those above them; the "go-fers" ("gophers") who "step and fetch it," or who function in the mail room; and finally at the bottom, those who handle the filth, the eliminative functions, janitors and sewer workers, untouchables.

The levels in the corporate body are levels of power and value. To mix the upper and the lower is to pollute, or to be polluted. To mix the higher intellectual and spiritual functions with the lower grasping and acquisitive ones, or with the lower sexual and excretory ones, is to profoundly pollute or be polluted—it is to be desecrated. It is terrifying anathema.

We exist as reacting, experiencing, and interpreting organisms within energies circulating through us and the rest of reality, our environments. What we immediately sense (I don't say perceive) are electrochemical events within each of our brains. But—of fundamental importance—our brains function within bodies conditioned and formed in mimetic engulfment with others in our home environments. If this were not so, we individual bodies with our individual brains could not refer to the same things, we could not live in a shared world-experienced. Sanity would be impossible. (For note, the brute immediate qualities of one person's experiencing do very likely, and in some cases certainly, differ to various degrees from another's: for but one example, color blindness.) And both the bodies of individuals and the group's corporate body are structured hierarchically into levels of power and value that all agree must not be blurred or mixed.

The metaphor of the corporate body doesn't merely illustrate what we already know, but helps us discover things we wouldn't have discovered otherwise. It helps us both to predict (perhaps) and to retrodict genocidal events, and, in general, to account for them.

Now let us extend the metaphor. What happens when our home group is shaky and we fear we *cannot stand up to* the other group? On the immediate, heated level of experiencing that I am trying to disclose, members are caught up in their home corporate body. And corporate bodies may threaten to smear into other, incompatible corporate bodies. The home group threatens to wilt and to smear into the alien group's way of being and experiencing. The home group's world-experienced trembles beneath them. Particularly horrifying for them is the prospect of smearing into the alien corporate body's lower regions.

Nobody is thinking, in any of the usual, honorific senses of that term. Two corporate bodies do not "smell right" to each other. This may be due to a divergence of behavior on a level that the reflective intellect—if it were operating—would regard as insignificant. Some difference in hygienic matters, or culinary, or what counts as acceptable physical distance in social interaction, or such. But immediately, as the corporate bodies threaten to rub up against each other, the difference between them radiates in a kind of nauseating panic throughout the corporate bodies and their members. Particularly disturbed, of course, is the shakier group.

Let us focus on especially provocative differences between corporate bodies: on matters of hygiene. Hitler inflamed his followers by blaming Jewish bankers for exacerbating the economic woes of Germany after World War I. He blamed their love of "filthy lucre." It may be no coincidence that just before this time Sigmund Freud and Karl Abraham were formulating ideas that equated money and feces on the subconscious level of minding. Briefly, the infant in toilet training exchanges his bowel movements for praise from his caregivers. Or again, he may refuse to move his bowels because he's holding out for a larger reward; he "hoards his treasure." A truly primitive struggle for power occurs.

Now notice how these ideas fit in with those pertaining to individual and corporate bodies, and the different levels of value, from the top down.

Hitler said such things as, "The filthy Jews' money grubbing hands are taking food out of our mouths." He was not saying that they were merely depriving good Germans of food! That doesn't begin to communicate the offensiveness and violation he was attributing to Jews. He was saying they were mixing the lower levels of body, specifically the excretory functions, with one's noble mouth, face, head.

Moreover, it was *their* excrement. No mix could be more polluting. He was charging Jews with an inexpressibly nauseating violation of non-Jewish Germans. This was the sort of charge that would incite many more-or-less ordinary Germans to genocidal mayhem. And would incite many professionals and intellectuals to systematic, cold blooded, mass murder.

Here is the keystone in the arch of my hypothesis concerning genocide: The brain is not a sealed, atomlike thing. It functions as a stage in surging brain-body-environment loops of energy exchange. *The brain functions in human bodies caught up in frequent and habitual mimetic contagion.* This contagion bonds individuals in their home group: and when this group begins to crack, members are terrified that they will be sucked into the alien group's way of being in the world. They fear that their corporate body will wilt in the face of the other corporate one, and that theirs will sink into the other's excretory level. They fear they will be annihilated.

When we function on this utterly prereflective and primal level, we don't make the distinctions that we take to be clear and fundamental when we are somewhat detached and able to reflect. We don't calmly and neatly say, "This is our group, that's the other group. We can keep to our path, they can keep to theirs." Particularly if our group is already shaky and vulnerable, we are, as I said, in danger of picking up mimetically on the other group's way of experiencing the world. This does not jibe with our deeply trusted, habitually experienced being and world. This is the ugly, stomach-turning dissonance which we experience immediately as, Their way of being is unassimilable! They must be expelled; they must be exterminated.

Quite a few have maintained that "projection" and "scapegoating" are going on in genocide. That is, that a group's destructive tendencies, for example, cannot be faced by that group, so they are projected onto an alien group: that group is blamed for aggression; it is scapegoated. This is importantly true.

But greatly ironically, we may conclude prematurely that our investigation into the causes of genocide is finished, that we grasp what makes genocide possible. But what if we haven't understood yet what makes projection and scapegoating themselves possible?

It is all too easy to form a visual image of persons as self-enclosed entities, something like fortified block-houses with slits in them, through which are projected beams of blame onto other, alien, self-enclosed entities. This suggests that the person-entities doing the projecting are self-enclosed and self-reflecting; and that they send out the beams deliberately, knowing just what they are doing.

These easy images disastrously mislead. For the facts of genocide vividly indicate that individuals are caught up in surging waves of group hysteria. Hence the key concepts—projection, scapegoating, individual—must be rooted in a completely different, non-entitative and non-atomistic context of thought. This will be a context in which our very being consists in how we are interlaced with, or better, interfused with others. Both others in the home group and others in the alien: though typically attractively and moltenly with others in the home group, and, in genocidal situations, repellently bound to others in the alien group (as if we were being strangled and are trying to escape). I argue that projection and scapegoating are pre-reflective, entranced, orgiastic group phenomena in which beings we call individuals participate—participate as extraordinarily vulnerable larvae, if you will.

The same word that appears in "individual person" appears also in "individual stone." But the stone is the stone whether anyone recognizes it to be the stone or not. While Barbara's or Joe's or Sam's identity is a function of how each is treated by others. Particularly how they are recognized, or fail to be recognized, by others. Identity is a function also of how they respond to this treatment.

Identity is a matter of our reality. We have all been infants. We are more vulnerable, more subject to suffering, even as adults, than we typically dare to imagine. Human suffering is inestimable.

We are born into what Don Miguel Ruiz calls "the planetary dream of suffering" (*The Four Agreements,* San Rafael, CA: Amber-Allen Publishing, 2000). This dream is constant and contrastless, hence seems absolutely normal and wakeful. Humans are so threatened by suffering that, awake or asleep, we see its potential sources everywhere. Terrible apprehension and blame spread like wildfires, and members of threatened groups live choked in smoke. (And which groups have never been threatened?) The planetary dream of suffering is the world-as-experienced by and through the culture into which we bodily beings happen to have been born, and which is unquestionable for us—"the way the world is." The dream is the particular form of intercorporeality and communal symbolization in which we try to support each other against threats to our existence, real or imagined. "If we could just get rid of *them,* everything would be OK." Projection, blame, scapegoating, madness.

Is there any escape from the planetary dream of suffering? That depends on whether we can come to terms with our vulnerable bodily being and our suffering *in its actuality*—not as dreamed. If we can, suffering will take its place within the whole picture. Its ever present possibility will not color everything in a pulsing, menacing smear of "World!"

When we deny that our bodies are ourselves, the experiencing body protests and takes revenge. Attempting to protect itself, it spreads itself in the miasmic, troubled smear through the world-experienced-by-it. As if it were screaming hysterically, "Notice me, Notice me!" This is the life of the damned.

To break the dream of suffering, we must awaken to the Nature that formed us—and stay awake. For there is not only suffering. There can be exultation to be alive for yet another day. What Albert Einstein called the miracle of the existence of the universe comes to full fruition only in and through ourselves, only in and through our exultation and wonder and gratitude. There is not only the possibility of suffering, but also the possibility of celebrating the universe and our tiny but vital place within it. Perhaps we can realize that how the world looks to us is largely a matter of how we habitually choose to look at it.

The account of genocide here presented might be called the pollution or infection hypothesis. One measure of its intellectual or dialectical power would be whether it makes some sense of a wide range of cases, ones closely and ones distantly related to genocide. That is, at least some of the conditions for genocide are very broadly operative in human behavior most of the time: they must be basic to human life.

Take shunning of any individual by any home group, for example, whether or not the group is genocidal. People are shunned because they are accounted unworthy of membership in the group for some reason. What might appear to the casual observer as apparently mild cases, are not so mild to those who are shunned! The phenomenon appears in starkest form with Australian Aborigines. Individuals who are thought to have become unworthy of membership in the group are shunned, exiled. They are ceremonially "sung out of existence," and typically they die quite soon.

Now note how a key feature of the pollution hypothesis—the surprising power of the head of a group—throws light on a case that is not exactly genocide, but it is related to it through this key feature. A stark example is the old Aztec practice of sacrificing humans to the head of the cosmos, the sun god, to appease his hunger for blood, for life. Thus the universe was kept going, so it was believed. As I understand it, only the best were sacrificed: the young, the fit, the strong, the beautiful. True, these victims were typically drawn from alien groups. But only the best of them were good enough for the god. For genocide to occur, an attempt would have to be made to kill or radically displace all members of an alien group.

Finally, salient features of the pollution hypothesis throw light on situations that seem, at first sight, utterly removed from the hysterical mayhem of genocidal purges. Take the usually cool atmosphere of academia. A professor at a branch campus of a large university is often deemed unworthy regardless of his or her intellectual accomplishments. Or, close to home now, professors of philosophy who do not tread the straight and narrow analytic path may very well be shunned, slighted, and may very well feel themselves to be invisible. It would, of course, be wanton stretching and weakening of concepts to call this genociding for the genteel. Nevertheless, a key feature of genocide is brought into clear relief: the power of mimetic engulfment in the central group, and the besmirchment, disparagement, or destruction of alien groups.

Is there hope for the human race? Maybe. By better understanding what we do in certain stressful situations, we may be able to block or divert genocidal tendencies before they are acted out beyond recall. We may better understand how humans often panic when faced with otherness in dangerous situations. We might learn to be less rigidly hierarchical in our home groups, to be less committed to a single, imperious head of our corporate body. (Here we might learn from thousands of generations of our hunter-gatherer forebears: there are different bosses in different situations. The boss is temporary; the boss is the one most competent to deal with a particular problem or opportunity. There is much of what we call today separation of powers.)

In general, there is hope if we can learn to stretch the bounds of what we find experienceable. If we can learn to imagine and to anticipate new and other forms of otherness. For all I know, this may be what the human race is trying, however fumblingly, to accomplish in the spate of extraterrestrial creatures to which science fiction and electronic games are treating us. The test will be how flexible we can be in actual situations under great stress.

There may be hope if we can achieve what Henry Bugbee in *The Inward Morning* said he was trying to win: to feel at home in the unknown.

It is hard to bring this essay to neat closure. I thought the last sentence might do it. But no, essential as that sentence is. All argument, all dialectics, even that which led to that sentence, is inadequate when we confront the unspeakable sickness of genocide. Finally, we must be open to a way of being other than the strictly intellectual or dialectical. I will leave it to Gabriel Marcel to suggest what it is:

> Consolation, which is a grace, is beyond all dialectics; the dialectician cannot understand it or even admit its existence, and consolation can easily become for him a mere object of derision. And yet, in a world such as ours, when suffering surpasses all estimation, it is the one who consoles who has the last word, unless it were to come from an absolute nihilist. Between consolation and nihilism, there is room only for conceptual games, which could not deceive the heart in any case.[5]

Notes

1. Norbert Elias, *The Civilizing Process* translated by Edmund Jephcott (New York: Urizen Books, trans., 1978 [1939], p. 196.

2. As previously noted, this essay is a *precis* of a book-length manuscript: *Making the World Pure for God: Genocide, Terrorism, and Human Nature.*

3. Bruce Wilshire, *Role Playing and Identity: The Limits of Theatre as Metaphor* (Bloomington: Indiana University Press, 1991 [1982]), indexed under "mimetic behavior."

4. Ernst Cassirer, *The Philosophy of Symbolic Forms*, vol. II *Mythic Thought*, (New Haven and London: Yale University Press, 1955).

5. This is Marcel's response to Bugbee, in *The Philosophy of Gabriel Marcel, The Library of Living Philosophers* (La Salle, IL: Open Court Publishing, 1984), p. 98.

7

Henry Bugbee:
Philosopher of Intimacy

Perhaps we can learn most from Henry Bugbee by learning why his dismissal from Harvard after five years as assistant professor was inevitable. One professor, knowing his quality, bid him goodbye with tears in his eyes. "But Henry, you haven't published enough." (Edward Mooney has apprised me of key events in Bugbee's life) Bugbee might have cited Socrates' apprehensiveness over the adoption of writing in Athens: he feared that people would rely on that which is written, and would no longer call things to remembrance within themselves; they would have forgetfulness implanted in their souls.

But probably Bugbee was too modest and too much his own person to compare himself to Socrates. Moreover, he does not seem to have been bitter at all on leaving Harvard, only thanking the department for giving him time in a stimulating environment to learn what his way of thinking was. Some years later appeared his only book-length published work: *The Inward Morning: A Philosophical Exploration in Journal Form*.[1]

There's something preliterate, prelinear, almost prehistoric and bardic about Bugbee. In key ways he resembles a Native American chief. He once told an interviewer about running away from home in Bronxville New York at age six and finding his totem animal: a fish, a goldfish, swimming in a pond. Yes, Bugbee comes as a rude shock to all that is advanced, refined, professional in the world of academic philosophy today. It is a world obsessed with publishing. And he prompts a fierce and most likely an aghast reappraisal of the ossified assumptions of that world.

In sitting down to write, don't we tend to assume that "we can get it all down"? Don't we assume that at least in principle there's a finite list of sorts that things can be, and that, in principle, we and others can sort it all out, given enough time? As we look back over what many consider the triumphant history of the West, doesn't it seem that this belief in the knowability of the world has justified itself many hundreds of times over? Of course, we do see quite a few thinkers covering their bets, adopting a fallback position: "Well, things are just what they are, right? And these whats must be graspable—if not by us, then by some mind somewhere, maybe God!" But, of course, the same broad assumption of the knowability of the world is again at work.

Before Bugbee began to publish his few, precious philosophical explorations (many of them in *The Inward Morning*) he had served as the captain of a ship in the second world war. He writes of Japanese Kamakazee pilots flinging themselves and their planes at U.S. shipping, and welcoming certain death. He seems to ask, Is what's going on knowable? Much earlier he had recognized his totem animal, the fish, and felt it mobilize him to the roots of his hair and the bottom of his feet. But is what's going on knowable?

Much links Henry Bugbee and Ernest Hemingway. First, their suspicion of all specialists, scientific or academic. (Of course, with this they share a trait with Tolstoy.) Second, their preternatural concentration on what's actually present in the sensorial life, their aversion to sweeping categories of thought and to abstractions. Socrates also had seen life and death at close range, as had Bugbee and Hemingway; none of them paraded their GRE and SAT scores. All three thought with an intensity that says, My life depends upon this.

Bugbee is explicit: he struggles and slips and slides in order "to find himself in the unknown." Socrates' last words are telling: he says he owes a sacrifice to the god of healing, Asclepius. For indeed the great mind, Socrates, knows that something is awry and that something must be healed. What could it be but intractable, tragic ignorance?

Hemingway finds relief from agony in a story: "A Clean Well-Lighted Place." Yes, in this cafe there's a place for everything, and everything is in its place, and it's all well lit and clean. And then what finally comes into view? Nothing, nothingness, that is, nothing in particular. We cannot know just *what* it is we cannot know, of course, but *that* it is is overwhelmingly evident to anyone who can stand the sight.

For there is what we know and know that we know. There is what we know that we don't know. And then, yes, there's what we don't know we don't know. It seeps and bubbles in from all sides around the edges of our tabulations and classifications, and through the cracks. Nothing. Nothing we can name. The courageous know it is inescapable.

For Hemingway, nothingness takes the form of blasphemy. The propped-up God, rigged to plug the holes and fill the margins and horizons in the alleged knowability of the world, collapses as nothingness courses in. Hemingway writes in "A Clean Well-Lighted Place":

> Our nada who art in nada, nada be thy name thy kingdom nada thy will be nada in nada as it is in nada. Give us this nada our daily nada and nada us our nadas and nada us not into nada but deliver us from nada; pues nada. Hail nothing full of nothing, nothing is with thee.

Just how would Socrates make his sacrifice to the god of healing, or ask others to do it for him? I don't know. The realization of the nothingness of what we don't know we don't know sets to sea all our schemes of categories and classifications, and sets thinkers back into themselves with a freedom and cleanness of slate that's the most individual thing in the world. And perhaps the most enlivening and scariest. Nobody but I am experiencing this now! Whether on the boat or in the sea water or half way in or half way out, each thinker is incredibly free and individual. Gertrude Stein in *Geography and Plays* (New York: Somthing Else Press, 1968) finds humor:

> He is suffering, he is hoping he is succeeding in saying that anything is something . . . He is hoping he is succeeding in hoping that something is something . . . He is hoping that he is succeeding in saying that something is something.

Oh, the fun, the fun: the jester straight-jacketed in subject and predicate!

Oscar Wilde likewise finds humor, piquant, marvelous humor. He gives this line to a fop in "Lady Windermere's Fan:"

> Life is far too important a matter to be talked about seriously.

At this point, a Buddhist might very well allude to the fertile void, or a Taoist to the marvelous Tao that cannot be said. And Bugbee? He gives us his incomparable self, and in the process begins to release each of us to each's incomparable self. For what happens when the ambitions and automatisms of Western thought begin to be evident and begin to fall apart? What happens when we cease to be held mindlessly in the assumption that everything in principle can be known and said? When we suddenly cease to believe that everything can in principle be objectified, set out before us in some conceptual or classifactory scheme or other purveyed by some authority or other, probably predicted? When we see with Bugbee (and William James) that every concept and every metaphor is "good for so much and not a bit more"?

What happens when we see our own clean well-lighted places? When, for example, we see the American Philosophical Association and its ruling analytic philosophers straightfacedly claiming to know who is the best philosopher of language, who the second best; the best epistemologist, the second best. The best graduate department of philosophy, the second and third best, etc., etc.

And let's bring it closer to home: For a clean well lighted place, take a program committee or executive committee meeting of SPEP, that is, the Society for Phenomenology and Existential Philosophy (Bugbee belongs in this tradition if he belongs anywhere). The questions are set: Has every representative of every oppressed group who might conceivably have something to say been included in the program? And certainly there is value in this, but . . . Has every drop that might conceivably be wrung out of Levinas been wrung? (Marcel, Hocking, Bugbee, James, Ortega, Thoreau, Emerson who are they?) And certainly there are drops to be wrung, but . . . What name can we fly here over the Atlantic so that the epigone can bask in reflected glory? Yes, to be sure, a place for everything and everything in its place.

And the effect? Found, I think, is an antidote to our dread of being our incomparable individual selves: our dread of the void and of nothingness. We don't see we cut ourselves off at the feet and are being propped up. In the case of SPEP—now caught up in "Continental philosophy"—it's transparent to anyone who can stand to see. The apparently exhaustive dichotomous classification, Continental or analytic? is not exhaustive at all. For it occludes a huge third alternative: ourselves, and our own New World creators in phenomenological and existential thought.

And Bugbee is certainly one of these—indeed, because of his uniqueness. His gift is to catch our attention when we are about to be frozen yet again in some stance of objectification and classification, one that overlooks our own feet and our own ground and land, and our own freedom even now to take an indefinite number of stances and attitudes. Bugbee:

There is this bathing in fluent reality which resolves mental fixations and suggests that our manner of taking things has been staggeringly a matter of habituation. Metaphysical thinking must rise with the earliest dawn, the very dawn of things themselves. [52]

Typically we are pre-set to objectify and catalogue the world in a certain way, so that everything looks inevitable, including our own cataloguing. But what if we were caught before being frozen yet again in some habitual stance of objectification and classification? What if new possibilities broke through the old, ossified ways of thinking and being, the same old noontime boredom, bleariness, *acedia?* Well, we would be living afresh, living in the earliest dawn, the very dawn of things themselves, that is, things as experienceable by us, as meaningful. We would not be able to give reasons for this, for reasons giveable reside in the old way of thinking and being. What Bugbee calls "true affirmation" is anterior to all reasons, though it may generate in time new ways of being reasonable. The earliest dawn is

. . . earlier than the day of morality and immorality. . . . No reason for acting can supplant the depth of true affirmation. This is not to disqualify the giving of reasons, or the having of reasons for acting; it is only to suggest the relative force of reasons had or given. [52]

Bugbee delineates sharply a leap of faith in the creative and regenerative cosmos that has formed us and that holds us each instant. For a leap of some kind at some time—or a stumbling lunge or a long forgotten stride—has in fact always been made by each of us. No one—not ourselves, not our parents or siblings—really knows us, each in our pulsing and piercing actuality. But people think they do, and we mimetic beings pick up unwittingly from them. We are dulled into some precommitment to possibilities that slants and limits all that the world can ever be experienceable by each of us as being. Other possibilities are concealed, and the concealment is concealed. The earliest dawn is a rebirth unimaginable before it happens.

So how is it ever to happen? Seductions and shocks. Seductions and shocks administered someway, somehow, by somebody or some thing. Maybe through what Bugbee (and Marcel) call rumination, so like the tilling of soil, when the damndest things turn up; and hopefully stay turned up long enough to be registered, before the groundless ground covers them over again. The universe is creating and maintaining each of us constantly beyond anyone's ability to comprehend it. In Spinoza's terms we exist within the roiling nexus, Nature creating–Nature created.

This is keenly suggestive but too abstract for Bugbee. Moreover, it lacks the bite of primal freedom. Waking up, he invokes his totem animal, the fish. Bugbee recounts fishing for steelhead trout in a river among the redwoods of northern California. A steelhead leaps into the air:

> It is a glorious thing to know the pool is alive with these glancing, diving, finning fish. But at such moments it is well to make an offering in one's heart to the still hour in the redwoods ascending into the sky. . . . Now the river is the unborn, and the sudden fish is just the newborn—whole, entire, complete, individual and universal. . . . To respect things qua existing, may indeed be *vision,* but it is vision *enacted,* a "seeing with the eye of faith." At its heart existence and decision interlock. One is himself the leaping trout [86, 130].

The grave problem with obeying Apollo's command, Know thyself, cited by Socrates, is that we are each of us too close to ourselves to be readily seen by ourselves. There is the taste of ourselves spread uniformly through everything anywhere experienced by us. But it is constant and contrastless, invisible. I repeat: On one level of analysis, the world sensed immediately (I don't say perceived) is a region of electrochemical activity in each of our brains. Our brains and bodies are individual, yet they have been profoundly mimetically conditioned over the years by other, authoritative bodies. How is it possible to thematize, acknowledge, express our continuous individual and communal slanting and limiting of our world-experienced? How possible to emerge from this sloth and stupor, this probable despair or fear unconscious of itself?

In this essay I am trying to gather clues. Through seduction and shock—say the shock of the newborn fish emerging from the unborn water. The fish experienced in the integrity of the experiencer's immediacy is experienced to *be* that experiencer!—that's what Bugbee says. Hemingway helps us by pointing to the unborn, the nothingness of what we don't know we don't know. "Some lived in it and never felt it but he knew it . . ." Out of this abiding unborn a new birth might occur—in those who need the cafe. Socrates helps us to understand with the sacrifice he asks his friends to make for him. We each must imagine just what that would be.

For Spinoza the rationalist, the nexus of Nature creating–Nature created is roiling. For Bugbee, and I suppose for most of us, the nexus is roiling and turbid. It may confuse and frighten us. We must discover a vaster and a deeper, an aboriginal, mode of reasoning which employs the bite of the totem animal. And which, I believe, is often led by music, as Schopenhauer and Nietzsche and Socrates knew. Bugbee:

> As true stillness comes upon us, we hear, we hear, and we learn that our whole lives may have the character of finding that anthem which would be native to our own tongue, and which alone can be the true answer for each of us to the questioning, the calling, the demand for ultimate reckoning which devolves upon us. [25–26]

Just when, how, where do we hear the anthem? Or, to return to the fish, when, how, where, do we see the leaping steelhead? As I recall, an incident occurred some years ago on the campaign trail. Walter Mondale, I believe, accused Gary Hart of vacuity. He challengingly asked, Where's the beef? So Albert Borgmann in an article on Bugbee, asks, in effect, Where's the trout?[2] Is this a rebuke, a lament, a cry of terror? Perhaps all three?

We no longer participate intimately and reliably in a universe creating itself out of itself every instant, Natura Naturans–Natura Naturata. A universe that is both God and Nature. Borgmann writes, "Bugbee realizes that finite being can warrant our testimony only in the 'sacramental act, and the sacredness of all things'."[3] But how are we to pin down the meaning of "sacramental act, and the sacredness of all things"?

We have a few clues. In working toward closing, let us try for a few more. Bugbee explodes the illusion of detachment. We are in the world over our heads, inescapably biased and slanted, and in more ways than we can imagine. "At its heart, existence and decision interlock," he writes. So why not try to make our commitments explicit? Why not use our resources in making vows? Why not vow in a "spirit of prayer," so that one vows to be "at the disposal of what we cannot command." [70, 81] Only in a decision to sacrifice power-over things can the "sacredness of all things" present itself. Only then can we live fully and spontaneously, each in his or her unplumbable center.

Moreover, Bugbee converges with an ancient tradition, typified, for example, in Plato and Emerson: Being or reality is found to be inherently valuable, that is, found to be of both de facto and de jure significance. One is moved to believe and feel that it is right that we exist. Part and parcel of this primal rightness is that we feel impelled to affirm this before we can give reasons for doing so. Likewise with the "demand for ultimate reckoning which devolves upon us," a demand that we give an account of ourselves. Part and parcel of the rightness of the demand is that we needn't support with reasons the demand itself. We simply vow to be at the disposal of what we cannot command. In this sacrificial act—for that is what it is—the sacred all-togetherness of things begins to appear. Now, how do we weave this presence into the everydayness of our lives as individual and communal beings today?

Bugbee gives us a clue that pertains to the factual and ethical truth of our being. Consider his account of a near calamity on a beautiful day on the North Fork of the Trinity River in California. Bright sun streams down from the tops of pines, people bask by a marvelous pool, and the roar of the rapids below "might have been but a ground-bass of contentment filling us all" [172].

There came a cry for help, seconded with a cry of fright. A young man flails at the tail of the pool, then is sucked under a huge log, and is carried down into the rapids. He bobs up for a moment, but there seemed no avoiding "an impending execution on the rocks below." Desperately he grabs at a willow's drooping branch, holds, and is carried in a wide arc toward shore. Bugbee:

> He had barely the strength and the breath to claw himself up on the muddy slope onto firmament. . . . I had run across the log and arrived on the opposite side below the willow, where he now paused, panting and on all fours, unable to rise. Slowly he raised his head and we looked into each other's eyes. . . . Not a word passed between us. As nearly as I can relive the matter, the compassion I felt with this man gave way into awe and respect for what I witnessed in him. He seemed absolutely clean. In that steady gaze of his I met reality point blank, filtered and distilled as the purity of a man.

The reality is the unspeakable preciousness of life, the cleanness is the absence in the boy of any pretense whatsoever.

In the integrity of immediacy what we hear when we hear a cry for help is, You there help me! Bugbee heeds the call, and what he receives is an experience of the unspeakable preciousness of life, of that life, and of any life.

But we exist in everydayness, hour by hour, day by day. We tend to relapse into egoistic stupor. The only thing that resembles perpetual enlivening shock and alarm are rituals imprinting and reimprinting in believers the preciousness of life and the sacred alltogetherness of things each instant. And it is just time-tested rituals of this sort that our secular society, ever spreading its influence, so woefully lacks.

There are some hopeful signs, however. A deep desire to be clean, to be truthful animates many people, leading them into encounter groups, etc. Likewise a deep desire to return to the regenerative cycles of Nature that formed our human species and prehuman ones, leads people into projects of ecological restoration of polluted and otherwise deranged environments. And, too, the plague of addictions can be understood—and in some sectors is understood—as shortcircuitings of the regenerative cycles of Nature (see my *Wild Hunger*).[4] We *might* recover from them! Finally, on this short list of hopeful signs, are the concerted and effective efforts, mainly in Europe, to curb the precipitous and shortsighted purveying of genetically engineered foods, and to guard against clonings of the most anarchic kinds.

But it is practically impossible to overestimate the destructive effects of what Gabriel Marcel called "the broken world," and Friedrich Schiller "the disenchantment of the world." Bugbee may have harbored no animus against Harvard for denying him tenure. But the rest of us should regard this with a shudder. Big words, like "sacred" and "sacrificed," have been emptied out society wide. Harvard is no exception—it flows in the lemming tide. Philosophy departments of "the best sort" are, on the whole, places for Cartesian mock battles, closets lined with mirrors instead of openings onto wild places. Closets instead of places into which to launch forays into what William James called "the unpent wilderness of truth," which phrase Henry Bugbee might also have used (perhaps he did, some place). It is not just religious fanatics who closet themselves, but smugly secular and scientist zealots as well.

We porous, vulnerable, essentially mimetic beings are left mainly to our own devices. A brush with nothingness and the unknown unknown might set us back into our own incomparable individuality and the moment-by-moment preciousness of our lives and our truth. We might yet feel "the simple pair," as Bugbee put it, "life and death, as they are ever harbored, tremulously unspoken, behind all that we say" [11]. We might yet feel the excitement of our own individuality and our own primal freedom, and, along with this, our basal responsibility to ourselves and others to give an account of ourselves.

And what are our chances? I dare not try to say. What possibilities will we create? I don't know. Nobody knows. Do leaps of faith as leaps of expectancy help bring about the rejuvenation that might—just might—be expected? Maybe.

Borgmann writes in the article cited: "When all of us will finally get to see the leaping trout and renewal will come to redemption, God only knows." We could close with this as our question.

Or would it be better to close with a few lines from Hemingway's acceptance speech (given in absentia) for the Nobel prize? He says of the writer:

> [H]e does his work alone and if he is a good enough writer he must face eternity, or the lack of it, each day. . . . For a true writer each book should be a new beginning where he tries again for something that is beyond attainment. He should always try for something that has never been done. . . . Then sometimes with great luck he will succeed. . . . It is only because we have had such great writers in the past that a writer is driven far out past where he can go, out to where no one can help him.[5]

Notes

1. Bugbee's chief work is *The Inward Morning: A Philosophical Exploration in Journal Form,* first published 1958, with an introduction by Gabriel Marcel (State College, PA: Bald Eagle Press). Fourth printing 1999, with an added introduction by Edward F. Mooney (Athens, GA: University of Georgia Press). Page references are noted in brackets in my text.

2. The Albert Borgmann article, "Bugbee on Philosophy and Modernity, is found in *Wilderness and the Heart: Henry Bugbee's Philosophy of Place, Presence, and Memory,* edited by Edward F. Mooney (Athens, GA: The University of Georgia Press, 1999).

3. The page reference for Borgmann: 126.

4. My *Wild Hunger: The Primal Roots of Modern Addiction* (Lanham, MD: Rowman and Littlefield, 1998). Another of my essays "Henry Bugbee: The Inward Morning" can be found in my *The Primal Roots of American Philosophy: Pragmatism, Phenomenology, Native American Thought* (University Park: Penn State University Press, 2000).

5. The Hemingway Acceptance Speech can be found in the *Nobel Prize Library* (New York: Helvetica Press, Inc, 1971).

8

William James on the "Spiritual"

What do we expect to be different for our experience when we hear the word "spiritual" rather than another word?

I mean we today—or many of us at least. Expectation disintegrates, spreading its fragments all the way from escapist flights from body and earth to a resonating covenant with body, earth, sky. Only twice is the word "spiritual" indexed by James in *The Varieties of Religious Experience,* and it means merely intuition or judgment of value, with the value of anything not to be reduced merely to its origins.[1]

So if by "spiritual" we mean value for living—and if we look for this value with something of James's own nervous intensity and alertness—then nearly everything he wrote is spiritual. What for him has value for living is what keeps us expectant and enthralled within the actual and possible "excited significance of things," away from withering depression, boredom, and death.

In 1870, soon after earning an M.D. degree, James fell into paralyzing depression. Thomas Carlson tells me he was hospitalized for some period (the records are sealed and apparently will remain so). In *The Varieties* James describes his own experience, but feigns to transmit somebody else's:

> . . . Suddenly there fell upon me without any warning . . . a horrible fear of my own existence. Simultaneously there arose in my mind the image of an epileptic patient whom I had seen in the asylum. . . . He sat there like a sort of sculptured Egyptian cat or Peruvian mummy, moving nothing but his black eyes and looking absolutely non-human. . . . *That shape am I,* I felt, potentially. . . . It was as if something hitherto solid within my breast gave way entirely, and I became a mass of quivering fear. (Lecture VI, "The Sick Soul")

When not in the mental institution, James was confined to his parents' house for about a year. There the rest of his life took shape. He concluded that only possibility is powerful enough to deal with possibility. The possibility of collapse into paralysis—the sculptured cat—can be countered only by the possibility of resurgence, of new life.

During his training he had been saturated with nineteenth century medical materialism, the doctrine that when all the forces impinging on us from without and within are tallied, one and only one vector of behavior must result. This dogma contributed to his paralysis, and he began to pick it apart. He thought, What seduces us to think that we could ever know all the forces impinging upon us?

But the typical alternative, conventional ideas of freedom, were of little help to him. Because though at many moments we feel emphatically that we might do things other than the ones we wind up doing, this feeling cannot be verified: we cannot repeat that moment of decision and do something else. We can't turn back the clock.

The white heat of his crisis generated another possibility, a third alternative. As I've mentioned, James reasoned that *if* he were free, then, logically speaking, the first act of freedom should be to freely believe in his freedom! (Bugbee says much the same thing with "primal affirmation.")

This is the explosive logic of faith. Having begun to work it out, James got out of bed.

The rest, as they say, is history. And it's a history that time and again can be reviewed by us with ever new possibilities of insight into what "the spiritual" might concretely mean. The possibility of paralysis, of fall into the nonhuman, never entirely left him. It is this threat that prodded him into pushing the envelope, into exploring relentlessly the possibilities of the human. The painting that engrosses us is not one that omits the devil, but one, he wrote, in which the devil appears—thrashing, grasped by the neck.

His epochal attempt to found a natural scientific psychology, *The Principles of Psychology* (1890), could not subdue contrary possibilities of approach stewing within the body of the work itself. They broke out and opened up a new metaphysics of pure experience, or radical empiricism, which led him beyond anything he (and most others, then and now) could have thought. The possibility that there were more possibilities than could be grasped powered him until death at sixty-eight in 1910.

But let us take it a bit more gradually. In the 1897 "Will to Believe," he adumbrated the more obvious features of the logic of faith. When faced with certain options—momentous, live, and forced—there is no way that reason, commonly conceived, can guide us. For example, the mountain climber asks, Can I leap this chasm? All the facts upon which we might base a decision are not yet formed, so, of course, not known. And indeed, our ability to imagine all that might happen as a result of our decision is limited, and limited beyond our ability to know how limited.

The point: sometimes only the faith that we can do something supplies the explosive power necessary to do it. In these cases, the faith with which "I can" is pronounced within one's inwardness, its force and weight, creates the evidence that makes it true. "I can" is equivalent to "I vow."

Certain rationalists believe that believing without sufficient evidence already garnered to support the belief is some kind of sin. James retorts that any alleged principle of reason that blights the possibility of truths appearing—truths of our abilities, say—must be unreasonable.

In *The Varieties* his logic of faith is considerably deepened, deepened beyond what he wrote in "The Will to Believe," because what the *willing* is in the willing to believe is more richly described. Our inability to imagine the limits of what can be imagined turns into a fathomless expansion of possibility. We sense that, all around us, separated by the thinnest membrane, is the region of what we do not know we do not know. Of course we cannot know just *what* this may be, but we sense *that* it is. And of course we cannot imagine unimagined possibilities, nor shape an unimagined goal of fulfillment or salvation and then work toward that. We can only attend to our incompleteness and suffering and allow—will to allow— whatever curative or fulfilling agencies or tendencies there may be "working behind the scenes" to germinate and to move us into a more "organic ripening" than was before imaginable.

James writes, "Religion, whatever it is, is a man's total reaction upon life, so why not say that any total reaction upon life is a religion?" He affirms that any total reaction upon life is a religion—in the important generic sense. He goes on with his classic statement,

> Total reactions are different from casual reactions, and total attitudes are different from usual or professional attitudes. To get at them we must go behind the foreground of existence and reach down to that curious sense of the whole residual cosmos as an everlasting presence, intimate or alien, terrible or amusing, lovable or odious which in some degree every one possesses . . . [this] is the completest of all our answers to the question,

"What is the character of the universe in which we dwell?" (VRE, Lecture II, "Circumscription of the Topic")

This anticipates Heidegger's existential category of *Befindlichkeit,* or Mood, as disclosure: how we are found by the universe anterior to anything we as agents might find. This anticipates as well Dewey's idea of the quality of whole situations which holds and silently conditions all our inquiries, and all our reactions and initiatives. It is the deepest clue to James's "spirituality": a new development in his logic of faith. All we can say of our allowing the background—our allowing the release of "subconscious allies behind the scenes"—is that the "rearrangement towards which all these deeper forces tend is pretty surely definite, and definitely different from what [the person] consciously conceives and determines. It may consequently be interfered with (jammed as it were . . .) by his voluntary efforts slanting from the true direction." (VRE, Lecture IX, "Conversion")

What is contacted in this disclosure? Of course, he cannot say. On its "hither side" it may be his subconscious mind (meaning?); on the "farther" he can only say it is "the More." He returns us to an earthen-energic process to which we and our species belonged long before anything could belong to us, before anything could be attributed to our own efforts. If the split self is mended or the sick soul healed, that is all we need know about the process. We allow "the More"; and when it works, it works beyond our ability to know how it works. What James at the close of "On a Certain Blindness in Human Beings" called "the mysterious sensorial life" *is* mysterious.

There is a vast pile up of questions at the end of William James's life. Call them "spiritual" if you wish. Possibilities radiate out in every direction beyond reach, and have drawn in the most adventurous philosophers of this century: Husserl, Whitehead, Wittgenstein, Dewey, and by implication, Heidegger and Merleau-Ponty. Now we see Hilary Putnam caught up in James. The challenge as I see it is to begin again at what he concluded was the center of his thought—radical empiricism—and then at the point he left off at his death in 1910 to continue to develop it. His *radical* empiricism: the fastnesses of phenomena anterior to the very distinctions subject/object, self/other, mind/matter.

This prepares for his last work in which he attacked "vicious intellectualism," the belief that what is not explicitly included in the definition of something is excluded from that thing. He perceived that things belong to each other more intimately, interfusingly, "knowingly" in a way, than the conventional intellectualist logic of excluded middle and the partitioned world could ever imagine.

What explodes with the repudiation of vicious intellectualism? The most basic of all conventional ideas: that something quantified as "one" is as sealed off from something else denominated "one" as is the *number* one from the *number* two. That is, exploded is the idea that there are self-enclosed entities, the building blocks of the universe, autonomous or nearly so: most obviously that selves are discrete and exist over against other selves. But nothing is immune from his rejection of vicious intellectualism: even "space and time" themselves as ideas may soften up and transform into notions we can't now imagine. Not even after Einstein.

James' logic of faith prompts him to flirt seriously a year before his death with Gustav Fechner's idea of modes of awareness very different from that allowed by our own nervous systems—plant souls, animal souls, even Earth soul. He discards his own earlier conclusion that conscious states cannot be summed. Perhaps what we take to be the focus of our individual minds forms merely a bit of fringe within a vast cosmic processual minding. James opens the way to possibilities of intimate belongingness of things with each other that exceed our received modes of awareness, and that exceed our ideas of what knowledge can be. It should not surprise us that his work stimulated, for example, Niels Bohr, and through him, probably, Werner Heisenberg and John Bell.[2]

Gary Snyder writes in *The Old Ways* "The yogin is an experimenter. He experiments on himself. Yoga . . . related to the English 'yoke' . . . means to be at work, engaged. In India the distinction between philosopher and yogin was clearly and usefully made—even though sometimes the same individual could be both."[3] I think James was both. Moreover, he might lead us North Atlantic people to grasp something of indigenous shamanic practice and thought in which the healer—having himself or herself passed through a near-death experience and opened up by it—conducts regenerative powers that the "once born" or "healthy minded" do not conceive. How can the possibilities of life appear to us vividly if we have not known the immanence of death?

Finally, by "spiritual" we should not neglect to mean "spirit": the refusal to give up when something solid within our chests gives way, and we then allow more than we conceive to possess us. The chest reknitted may be stronger than the chest that broke. And we need have no idea why.

Notes

1. William James, *The Varieties of Religions Experience* (New York: New American Library, 1958 [1902].

2. See, for instance, Heisenberg quoting Bohr on James, in *Physics and Beyond*, New York: Harper Torch Books, 1972, 134–135.

3. San Francisco: City Lights Press, 1977, p. 11.

9

Looking for Bek

We nurse the child along, the delightful child, the young woman. First one thing is wrong, then another, and another. She's a serious singer and actress. She finds a coach who releases a startling new volume of sound. "It's coming from Bek?!" But his piano is out of tune and after some months she is singing off pitch. Et cetera.

But then, at nearly thirty, it all comes together in one bursting, flashing, ecstatic hour of accomplishment in July, 1995. Merkin Hall, near Lincoln Center, Manhattan. She takes command of the stage, she takes over the theatre. It's Bekah and Larry Woodard in an "Opera Bistro:" with talent to burn, they interlace and burn it in a blaze for all to see and hear. The other soprano reduces her numbers. We learned later that she complained of a strained voice.

Afterwards Donna and I stand and float in the lobby. She's surrounded. I am lauding Larry. I notice an old man standing against the wall, looking abashed, perhaps stricken. Later I learn who he is and that he was awestruck.

Arnold.

She cannot have coffee with us. She sits at a table with the other performers and with whatever agents or grandees happen to be here. I want to be with her. Instead of claiming her as mine—See! See!—I must let her move away into the world she is creating for herself. I am elated and forlorn, bubbly, ditzy, alone.

About a week later she tells us about Arnold Michaelis. She and her husband, Tim, have visited him in his apartment on Forty-fourth Street near the UN. She says, "He plays recordings of Arthur Grumiaux and Clara . . ." "Haskil," I interpose. "Yes, Haskil!" she says. And Arnold is very interested in her career. And who is Arnold? "Oh, he did something with Arnold Stevenson." ". . . Adlai Stevenson?" "Yes, that's it! He advised

Stevenson on his speech about the Bay of Pigs, or something like that, that he gave at the UN."

"And when might we meet Arnold?" "Yes, he wants to meet you and Mom. He said he'd like to have dinner at the Flower Drum around the corner from him on Second avenue."

I arrive in the restaurant on a night a week later (Donna parks our car). I approach the table where Rebekah sits with the man who must be Arnold. It was that old face again, now smiling warmly. I walk tall. I'm Bekah's father! He rises unsteadily and I greet him. "Arnold Michaelis, I presume?" (Too much like "Dr. Livingston, I presume," but too late to change that.) We sit and chat before the meal. He is "full of high sentence but a bit obtuse," I think, his voice a radio voice. I learn of his own music program on WNCN, the music station now defunct. I must have heard him many times. "For the Love of Music."

Afterward we go to his apartment. Dingy, dusty, one room, yellowish peeling walls, no bed. Bekah tells me later that he sleeps in the reclining chair. The walls are crammed with large glossy framed photos of himself and the great ones he has interviewed or worked with in some way: Nehru, King, Humphrey, several of Adlai Stevenson, Indira Ghandi, Bruno Walter, Coretta King, Chester Bowles, Eleanor Roosevelt. Remaining space is filled with tapes, tapes upon tapes, audio, VCR, music, interviews, and LPs. None of the photos is more recent than the early 1970s.

After each dinner at Flower Drum in the months that followed, he somehow communicated that he desperately wanted to pay, but couldn't. His mouth said he would, his eyes said he couldn't. We would, nearly always, pay and return for the ritual Grumiaux and Haskil in Mozart or Beethoven sonatas and his own coffee ice cream. Both Donna and I wished to hear some of his interviews. I wanted particularly to hear Bruno Walter's voice. Arnold never got around to it.

He could barely walk. One night, we learned, Bek came across and downtown at 2 A.M. to minister to his terrible pain. "He's so big across the back," she said. "I could hardly move him or do anything for him. I held him."

Gradually his radio voice faded from my awareness. "He's planning a concert of German lieder at the University of Georgia." (A concert of German lieder in Georgia? He will sing?!) Her mom and I and Bek and Tim arrive at a dinky apartment on an airshaft in the teens of Manhattan for the last rehearsal. An old friend of his—and old—accompanies him, and well. He stands with one hand braced on the piano.

He is eighty-two or three, has taught himself to sing by listening to Herman Prey recordings. His voice is a trifle unsteady but right on pitch and greatly disciplined and musical. Beethoven, "To the Distant Beloved." He asks me to translate some of the words. His German is better than mine and I stumble embarrassed and stop. Much later I wondered with a start if people had always been put off by my own radio voice.

Both her mother and I had come to New York some forty years earlier to conquer the mountain of New York theatre. We had only meager success. But now Bek had a good chance as a singing actress. Arnold kept intimating, sometimes promising, interviews with the great. He did get through to Robert Whitehead, the fabled producer, and Bekah got to meet his wife, Zoe Caldwell, in her dressing room after her fine enactment of Maria Callas. But no Robert Whitehead.

"From my seventies to eighties I was left for dead," Arnold said, "but I'm still alive!"

We hurry to Trinity Church, Wall Street and Broadway. She is a soloist there. Today, a week day, she is to sing Bach's Coffee Cantata. She sits with the baritone soloist. The choir director, Owen Burdick, is at the harpsichord. It has not quite begun. We're in time. Her mother's fragile hand grips mine almost tight enough to hurt. We always do this. She's a fusion of us, Donna and me. We don't really understand it, but she's a fusion of us, and our lives are suspended on each run and swoop and trill of her voice—a glinting tracery of sound in the air. She finishes one of her numbers. We breathe. Applause ripples through the old Gothic church. I burn and glow, I nearly expire with pride.

Her look as she sits there is the strangest I have ever seen on her face, an awed look, "Did I do that?" But it's somehow a sad look as well. She is a bit overweight and her heels are worn down. I didn't know why I noticed that.

Now it's several weeks later, about three weeks before Christmas, 1996. We were to pick up Arnold and drive downtown to hear Bekah and the choir sing the Messiah. But it's the traffic madness before Christmas. Bogged down on Canal Street, I park and phone him from a booth and beg off. He can't come on his own. "We'll visit you afterwards."

The singing is glorious, Bekah's two solos accomplished, sublime. We see her in a back room and I tell her we're to meet Arnold. "No, I want to relax with my friends." "OK . . . but you've got to phone Arnold and explain." She does so in the church. We walk to a flashy hotel bar. She sits with her friends and explains to me, "Arnold has a family of his own."

I am stunned. This is so completely unlike her. "Bekah shares," thus I had spoken of her and to her since childhood. I've never known anyone so generous. I could not have known then how tired she was.

She cooked Christmas dinner for us all in their half-finished Brooklyn loft. I sat right next to her and, without her make-up, she looked peaked and worn. A good cook, she overcooked the meat. I could not have known then how tired she was.

Neither she nor Arnold nor any of us could have known that in two weeks both would be dead.

On New Year's Day we pick up Arnold in our car. It's only about 100 yards to the Flower Drum, but he cannot walk. Painfully he begins to step into the car, but pauses with his foot on the door's opening and breathes deeply. "Ah, the air, the air."

A neighbor of his called us two days later. "Arnold has died." We did not know if Bekah had heard. She had not. A panicked rushing sound came over the phone line. She may have turned to tell Tim. "Oh . . . Oh . . . no," and a pause. In a small breathless voice, "You know what nearly happened to me on Sunday?"

We knew she had fallen from a spirited horse in Central Park. Her helmet had fallen off (not the one I bought her that snapped under her chin). Reaching for it, she fell and sprained her ankle badly. She walked back to the stable to see if the horse had made it through the streets.

She called us three days later, Saturday night. A long call, more forthcoming than ever before. "I love you, Mom and Dad."

She was still mainly sitting, and Tim would sometimes rub her leg. But she was to sing at Trinity the next day.

Sunday morning our son called. He sounded terrified. "Don't move, don't go anywhere! I'll drive over." He refused to give reasons. I called him, he refused. He is a physician and surgeon. I supposed that maybe he had killed someone on the operating table. I called our lawyer, left a message, and got dressed in coat and tie.

Then Tim called us. "I'm in a Brooklyn hospital emergency room. They've been trying to bring her back. They did a few times. They can't anymore. They've given up . . . maybe from the fall . . . "

I told Donna to sit down. She ran upstairs to the other phone, calling, Bekah, Bekah!!

Looking for Bek. For thirty-one and a half years she was with us, and of great stretches of it I have no memory at all. Seventy articles, nine books,

I was carefully creating worlds of words. Putting food on the table. Being a professor. But as homeless men and women on the streets of Manhattan mutter and talk to themselves, sometimes only their lips moving, so, I sometimes think, I have been talking to myself, trying to define myself, lost to her.

Looking for Bek. Only some high points of our relationship come back to me. Maybe in looking for her in these words (more words, but how else?), the blanks between will begin to fill in? When I explain it to you will they fill in?

In Antarctica, in Queen Maud's Land, some stray pinnacles of rock emerge like black teeth from a mile-deep sheet of ice and stick up another mile in the sky. But beneath the ice they are all one continent of Earth—all connected.

At the close of 1964 Donna is pregnant with our second child. My dissertation is coming along, but the end is not in sight. Since our first child in 1961, Donna has not worked in a money-making job. We're in public housing; but I am worried about funds. I call my mentor, William Barrett, and he encourages me not to worry. "Children are resilient," he says.

The child is due the middle of June. Given Donna's long torso, she doesn't bulge much, just thickens. The middle of June comes and goes with no labor, not the slightest tremor. By the middle of July old Mr. Katz who sits on the stoop of our project begins to pester Donna. "You told me it would happen in mid-June." By the first of August, his consternation rising, Donna, very thick, says, "I've decided not to have the child, Mr. Katz." This stymies him.

It is now mid-August, and no contractions, nothing. Donna and I eat Mexican food near the Empire State Building. Afterward we walk up Fifth Avenue about thirty blocks.

We fall asleep in our apartment around 11 P.M. (our son is visiting a friend's family on Long Island). I awaken about four. Donna is not in bed. I go into the bathroom. She is lying on the floor, curled up. "Gas," she says.

We hurriedly dress and get into a cab on Columbus Ave and go in short order to NYU hospital at Thirty-fourth and East River Drive. Someone called the obstetrician. Maybe I did. I sit perhaps an hour in the waiting room. The youngish and rugged looking doctor appears and says, "You've got a big girl."

I give him a bear hug and let loose a cry of thanksgiving. He quickly withdraws. Someone directs me to the newborn area and a nurse behind the glass holds up this nine-pound-plus infant girl, already with a lot of dark hair. As certain as I am sitting here writing this, I am sure that she looked into my eyes, looked as if she were gurgling, and turned away fetchingly.

Rebekah!

Her birth certificate read "Rebecca." No, I order, the spelling is wrong. It must be as found in the King James Bible, that's the one that's right.

Donna goes along with it. That's the way it was in those days.

The obstetrician believed she gestated eleven months. When he first saw Donna the first of November how could he have mistaken an empty womb for an occupied one?

Nobody I have ever known looked more at home in the water. Bek swam by undulating her body under the surface like a porpoise. I would kid her, "But can you swim like a human being?" She could, but didn't like to. Even as an infant when her diaper was wet she would seldom cry, but just coo in her crib in a sort of liquid way.

She developed some cradle cap, encrustations on the scalp. I actually took leave of my work, sat her in a pan of water in the sink in Indianapolis, and began to soften it and scrub it off. It took several sessions over two days. Only rarely would she wince or complain as she played in the pan full of warm water.

We moved back to the East when she was four. Once when she was about seven she and I drove down to the outer banks of North Carolina. We camped in the dunes in the sound of the surf. Just behind these dunes were ponds of fresh water. We fished there for small sunfish and bluegill. She caught one, and cried, "Bring a bucket, bring a bucket!" I was non-plussed. One either kept a fish and killed it or returned it to the water. But I ran to our camper and returned with a bucket. She said, "Good!," filled the bucket and watched the brightly colored fish finning in the dazzling water.

Her rapport with other living things was phenomenal. Her being-in-communion grew along with her. She (about eighteen at the time), my wife, and I were walking in the Lake Country of England. Noticing a horse in a pasture we stopped. Fortunate to see it at all, for it stood stock still under a tree, looking out at us from under boughs. All alone, it looked forsaken. Standing at the rail fence, my wife and I tried various appeals to lure the horse toward us. For several minutes this went on, the animal keeping its frozen stance, baneful and pitiful. Our daughter made a few little sounds in her throat and the horse came over.

When she was little she collected small animals, rabbits and abandoned cats and kittens. One apparently undistinguished rabbit was so handsomely groomed and nourished that the judge at the local fair created a special category for an award: General Rabbit. I referred to it as such at every opportunity.

Her cats roamed the house and formed our daughter's most intimate family, which amused me. But I did not relish them roaming our bedroom as we slept. So each night, however tired, I tracked them down and deposited them, a bit roughly at times, in the furnace room.

One of her cats, Charcoal—as undistinguished by all objective standards as any cat could be—became sick and emaciated. She dragged her hindquarters. Clearly she would die soon. One evening late, while all others slept, she looked up at me and made a sound. I found myself kneeling beside her and holding my head against hers. Astonished and elated, I said Goodbye.

When Rebekah was about thirteen, we were phoned at midnight and informed that she had been found passed out at surf's edge in New Jersey, about seventy miles from where we lived. A nearly empty bottle of Vodka lay beside her. When we arrived very early in the morning at the hospital she lay blearily on a sheetlike hammock. I looked urgently into her eyes and asked her, "What are you doing?!" She looked straight at me and blurted, "I'm just a little kid."

She implied that she would learn. And she did. But aided by removal from a circle of friends desperately seeking adulthood and not knowing the way. Distanced by thousands of miles, living with my youngest brother and his wife, she discovered the singing and music that would so distinguish her. Very likely, a deep memory lingered of her mother singing to her a lullaby every night before crib time. Earlier than that, nested in her mother's singing and dancing body, she must have heard singing and felt her mother's movement all through herself.

When she left to live in California I felt I was too busy to ride with Donna and her to the airport. As she stepped into the car a tear appeared in one of her eyes. Could I have been that busy?

Two years she was gone in California. I would often ride my bike many miles. Happening to pass a cemetery, I noticed a monument to a child inscribed, We miss you everywhere. Yes, that was it. She occupied a realm with animals and avian and marine things that circulated timelessly all around me wherever I went but never quite through me. It was a dreaming zone in which I was not secure. Just before she died I had said to her as I left their loft one night, "I miss you Bek." As if she were a visitor from some realm come to beckon me for a time and then depart.

Before our daughter's return to New Jersey we move twenty five miles north. We think this is far enough to avoid all but the most improbable encounters with her old friends.

She returns considerably changed. My sister-in-law is a strict disciplinarian, precisely what Bekah needed. (Only once did we feel the need to reinforce their care: when Bekah played hooky one day from school to visit the Santa Anita race track.)

Bekah had been enrolled in a Christian school, Maranatha, meaning, May Christ Return! We found a comparable school in our area, Timothy Christian. It was well-run, devout without being fanatical, with a head who was a computer whiz. Apparently, Bek took to most of her classes, and certainly to the computer. This would serve her later when she worked part time in Wall Street brokerage houses for twenty-six dollars an hour while pursuing her singing career. She graduated as salutatorian while finding time to consume gothic horror novels, science fiction, and *Anna Karenina*.

We also found an evangelical church nearby. She and her mother sang in the choir. I would often pray with her at night. I could sincerely pray. Look, if I had been exploring a cave and the one opening collapsed, I would have cried out—wouldn't I—whether I believed anyone could hear me or not. Wouldn't you? I prayed desperately for her and for us.

When she was about fifteen she and I drove together in our camper to Maine. We climbed Mount Katahdin, the most alpinelike mountain in the East, and it reminded us of two trips we had taken in the Sierras when she lived in California. Coming down, she outdistanced me and disappeared, beating me to camp by about half an hour.

We swam in Moosehead Lake. Once while returning to the camper while I lay on the sand she tossed her head and looked back at me fetchingly. The leather wings of desire rustled for a moment and then were quiet forever.

We sometimes read the Bible at night. She was curious about why we had named her Rebekah, and we read about that ancient woman and how she tricked old Isaac to give his blessing to the youngest son, Jacob, rather than to the eldest, Esau. "But why did you name me after *her?*" I did not know what to say. (I did not know at the time that ancient Rebekah was acting out of an immemorial matristic tradition still alive in her in which the mother's youngest child is the one who is blessed. She had not given up the battle with her husband, the patriarch.)

Soon the cruelties visited upon the Caananite people by Joshua and his troops were too much to stomach. We moved rapidly to the gospel of John and the epistles of John: "God is love."

But the fact was, I could not consistently enact the role of an evangelical Christian. Moreover, my own identity problems boiled over. I would often mutter, "Who am I, where am I, Why am I?" Yes, I would. Precisely what growing children do not need from their parents.

The fact was, neither my wife nor I could provide a stable framework for negotiating ritualistically the children's stages of development—rites of passage. They flew for confirmation to companions whose parents were as much in flux as ourselves. Culture clash between ancient Rebekah's matristic culture and Isaac's patriarchal one mirrors in some ways the clash of cultures in our time. But for many of us, traditions of any sort have collapsed almost totally.

Over one hundred thirty years ago Dostoevsky predicted the situation of so many of us "enlightened" and "intellectual" people. Again, speaking through the troubled Svidrigaelov in *Crime and Punishment,*

> Ah, . . . nowadays everything's all mixed up . . . we don't have any especially sacred traditions in our educated society; it's as if somebody patched something together the best he could out of books, one way or another, or extracted it out of the ancient chronicles. But those would be the scholars, and they're all blockheads . . .

I also feel an affinity with hapless Roskolnikov, who thought he was so bright and special that he could flout conventional standards, but learned that he was not so bright and special after all:

> I didn't believe. Yet I was hugging Mother just now, and we were crying. I don't believe. Yet I asked her to pray for me. God knows how it works . . . I don't understand any of it.

What I could give my children sincerely and more or less consistently was not enough, but it was not nothing: I could take them to the mountains and show them the ecstasy of endurance, and at night the sky blanketed with stars. We could get some sense together of the magnitude of the cosmos and our tiny but vital place within it. In later years Bekah's unstable knees prevented her from returning to the high mountains, but our son—buffeted by the vicissitudes of medical economics and reprieved for a moment—loved to go back and see the stars, "Just to know they're there." And Bekah even toward the end would answer to my greeting, "Sierra Bex!" Or, "Sierra Bex, the soup queen!" For when she was with us she was always the first to get the backpack butane stove running and water heating for soup as the sun went down behind the mountains and a sudden chill fell upon us.

Donna and I clung to each other in bed, as if a wound might heal if the sides of the lesion were pressed together long enough. Even people we hardly knew embraced us: it seemed as instinctive as the jerk of a knee when tapped with a rubber hammer. As if bodies are members of a more real corporate body out of which a common heart has been torn, and we press our bodies together for a few moments to restore the conviction that life still goes on.

Donna had a menstrual period again after a lapse of twelve years. Instinctively we had intercourse. Might there be one egg left, one?

I began teaching again two weeks later, the beginning of the spring semester. I ate very carefully and rested systematically before every class. It worked for the first two weeks. Not telling the students about our loss was like keeping Bekah's presence and being inside of me, which fueled me.

Then one day it didn't work. I had had early dinner and had gone to the car to rest in the reclining seat. I got up at five minutes before 6:00 and felt completely empty, the lassitude and despair overwhelming. I had to meet 240 undergraduates at 6:10. I walked toward the classroom, the same way for awhile as to the "grease trucks" where I could buy candy. Seriously hypoglycemic all my life, I knew that I would be high for twenty minutes, then plummet to emptiness, and be jittery, with a burning stomach, for the remaining hour with the students. At the point where the way branched off from the trucks I kept walking toward them. I asked myself, "Are you in charge of your life or aren't you?" I kept walking toward the trucks. Now only one hundred feet away, my face was prickly and hot. I kept walking. I had done such things for decades.

"Professor Wilshire!" I cried out to myself. Then, as if taking myself by the neck and turning my head, I broke through, and forced myself off the sidewalk and across the street toward the classroom.

The next weekend at a party a woman asked me what I did. I said I taught in a philosophy department. She asked, "What are you working on now?" A moment's panic: I had to tell her exactly and precisely that it was addiction I was working on, and how an addictive craving is ambiguous, is "both me and not me." I heard myself blurt, "it is, it is . . . a trance that has to be broken through. It is a TRANCE!" The relief was indescribable. She seemed to understand.

About another week later I recounted these incidents over the phone to my friend, Glen Mazis. "Is it in your book? It should be." Obvious, once he said it, but I had not thought to do it! Or could not, not so publicly and finally. I immediately wrote what you've just read.

Ezekiel 1:1–18 came to mind:

> I saw visions from God. . . . A strong wind came out of the north . . . and out of the midst of it . . . glowed amber metal, out of the midst of the fire. . . . As to the appearance of the wheels . . . a wheel within a wheel. . . . As for their rims, they were so high they were dreadful . . . and they were full of eyes round about.

Addicted life is a wheel that cannot imagine its limit, dares not imagine the wheels containing it, their rims of eyes reading and opening us to all, but which we cannot read. In what may I still be trapped?

I had been working on a book on addiction for nearly eight years. I had sent out versions of it for six years and been rejected by many publishers. I had begun to think that I was too old and beginning to lose my grip and that I had overreached my capacities. Others began to wonder as well.

I had now found the through-line of the book—the way to distinguish addictive cravings from normal hunger pangs. Addictive cravings are experienced as both mine and not mine, me and not me. They are crazy-makers. They throw us into entranced, semimechanical repetitions. Whereas a normal hunger pang may be unpleasant, but we know we can eat in a few hours and we respond intelligently.

The despair over Bekah's death was a gift from her, I believe. It forced me into a confrontation with myself I had always avoided. Now I must cut everything unnecessary, and think with an honesty and intensity that is worthy of her father, that can compensate a tiny bit for her loss. God help me.

We brace ourselves day by day to prevent falling into the abyss. We buried some of her ashes near the shore of Puget Sound, her husband's home, where they would go some day to settle down and have children. Many came there, and many more to her requiem at Trinity Church. Came from all over, the many people she touched deeply in her thirty one and a half years. A friend from Sarah Lawrence College days, Tamara Lindesay, came from England, and gave us this poem:

Birdsong

It was in Woolworth's in Yonkers,
before forty ruffled parakeets rattling their cage
in the pet department, that I first saw you sing.
It was as if you had flown through the door,
their long-lost mother brought back to them
in human form, to ease their restless fluttering,
bring them a moment of peace. And sure enough
within minutes, your singing had coaxed
each and every one of them to sleep.

I wonder if all those parakeets found
owners to love them, liberate them
from Woolworth's, bring them home,
give them names. Maybe they carried your song
on their travels, taught it to their children,
maybe it's known to birds all over New York.
I'd like to think they have the power
to conjure you here, your voice lingering
on the air for an instant, before it disappears.

Another friend from college, a tall woman like our daughter, told me at the requiem about skulking self-consciously on the periphery of a party one night. She related that Bekah sidled up to her and said, "Isn't it great to be tall!" The friend said, "It changed my life."

Last summer I was visiting my middle brother in California. He is an extraordinarily staid and self-contained academic historian. As I turned away to leave that night, he said, "I have something to tell you."

I had heard him talk for sixty years, but never in that tone of voice. I turned abruptly to see him smiling in an odd way. Afflicted with stuttering since childhood, nevertheless now he spoke fluently and calmly. He said, "I was gathering up exams in a large lecture hall, but thought a few students hadn't finished. Sometimes students will slump down in their chairs, perhaps pouring over a dictionary, trying hard to finish. I checked each row. There were no students left. Still, I believed someone was present in the room. I suddenly looked at something in the room and said, Bekah, is that you? Bekah, is that you? She seemed to be taken aback that I would doubt it. She said, Tell dad not to worry. She stood there a moment looking at me, and then was gone. . . . I thought you should hear about this. I didn't know her very well, but that's about what happened, as near as I can tell you."

Rebekah's mother-in-law, a quiet, unexcitable woman, told us of hiking near Zermatt Switzerland the next summer. She said she heard someone coming up behind her on a bicycle, and then, "It was Bekah. She flashed by me, saying, 'Isn't this fun!'"

Donna, returning from two weeks abroad, opened the front door of the house, and it was as if a wind swept past her and out of the house. "It was Bekah," her mother said.

Recently I was returning home in my car after a workout at the gym. I recalled a snapshot I had happened to see of myself as a young man holding Bekah on my knee. Just for a second it registered. (My wife happened to have the photo out; I couldn't bear seeing pictures of her.) She was perhaps five months old. The picture caught an expression of hers I remembered: an odd, old-woman's expression on her baby's face. Maybe she was a spirit-child, I now said to myself—trying to figure out what that could possibly mean.

Then I thought, She may be on the front porch waiting for me. I didn't believe it exactly. I didn't not believe it either. What I thought of—and my thought itself—were oddly placeless and timeless, a state of mind I never recall having before.

When I drove up the driveway, I was not surprised. She was not sitting on the porch. But something was on the porch. It was in the mailbox, an unexpected letter from our friend, Calvin Martin. My wife had sent him and his wife Tamara's poem. The letter read,

Nina keeps marveling that Bekah could calm those birds with her singing. More than that, that she would even *think* to do this, and that she would do it in a public place. This is an extraordinary person indeed.

Somebody with that kind of spirit doesn't die. Let me tell you emphatically: that spirit cannot die. I lived too long with Eskimos to think that people like this, like Bekah, merely come and go. No. They don't. These people house a spirit that is immortal, that is earthy. . . .

Something (I purposely use this mythic word, "something," to keep it unspecified, plenipotential, powerful—what in quantum language is known as "superposition") dwelled in her. The late poet and anthropologist Stanley Diamond said that writing a poem is like experiencing a mysterious arrow: it comes from somewhere we know not whence and passes right through us on its journey. . . .

But it had to continue on its trajectory. And so it did. But it is not gone, nor dead, nor even remote. It is there with those parakeets in Woolworths; it is there in the lives of her friends and those who heard her sing; it is there with you two and her husband and brother. It is out there on the dawn, there in the path of the moon . . .

I don't know if you understand what I'm saying. You mourn . . . imagining her death was trivial or accidental . . . It's like saying that the trivial and accidental would happen to Ulysses or Persephone or Diana—that it could happen to some being who housed the power of the universe . . .

It is now four years and five months since our daughter died. To my knowledge she made no more "reappearances" after five or six months. This agrees with certain indigenous people's observations that the soul lingers for a while in its wonted places and then departs. Which suggests that the bodies of the living—longing for the deceased and expecting her somehow—spontaneously, viscerally reproduced her body-self as that had interfused their own body-selves, flowing through them for so long. Something like a photographic negative that fades in time?

But I do feel her energy in my work. Strange sadness, strange excitement.

Dear, dear Bek.

ACKNOWLEDGMENTS

Professor John Stuhr, head of the Department of Philosophy at Penn State, shared with me the snippet of conversation between two Princeton graduate students (recounted in chapter one) that he overheard in an elevator at the APA convention in New York City in 2000. While we conversed about this appalling trend in the education of today's professional philosophers, the first essay began to catalyze in my head. I thank John—and Dame Fortune. I thank my old friend, Dr. Cedric Tarr, for acute conversations on political aspects of genocide. These led me to discern an X factor needed to explain the gruesome phenomenon, one that eludes all conventional modes of explanation, political, sociological, economic, etc. I also owe a debt of thanks to Professor Merrill Skaggs of Drew University who helped in many ways, one of which was coaching me in modulating the scatological aspects of my pollution theory of genocide so that it would be more acceptable to the general reader. In the dedication of this volume, I implicitly thanked my Pluralist colleagues in the APA, but I thank them again in this closing page. I thank my wife, Donna, who has supported me in every way, not the least of which is with her insights into archaic or primal experience, and into the abiding legacy of prehistory: the crucial role, even when unrecognized, of myth and ritual in our everyday experience. Finally, I thank her for helping to compose the index when I was running on empty.

INDEX